APPROACHING ALI

APPROACHING
ALI

*A Reclamation in
Three Acts*

Davis Miller

LIVERIGHT PUBLISHING CORPORATION

A DIVISION OF W. W. NORTON & COMPANY

Independent Publishers Since 1923

NEW YORK   LONDON

Aside from those brief chapters described as dream material,
Approaching Ali is a work of nonfiction.
Certain names and identifying details have been changed.

The chapter "My Dinner with Ali" was published in a much shorter form in *The Best American Sports Writing of the Century* (Houghton Mifflin), *The Beholder's Eye: America's Finest Personal Journalism* (Grove/Atlantic), and *The Muhammad Ali Reader* (Ecco Press). The chapters "The Zen of Muhammad Ali, Part One" and "The Zen of Muhammad Ali, Part Two" were published in a much shorter form in *The Best American Sports Writing, 1994* (Houghton Mifflin).

For information about permission to reproduce selections from this book,
write to Permissions, Liveright Publishing Corporation,
a division of W. W. Norton & Company, Inc.,
500 Fifth Avenue, New York, NY 10110

For information about special discounts for bulk purchases, please contact
W. W. Norton Special Sales at specialsales@wwnorton.com or 800-233-4830

Manufacturing by RR Donnelley Harrisonburg
Book design by Chris Welch
Production manager: Louise Mattarelliano

ISBN 978-1-63149-115-3

Liveright Publishing Corporation
500 Fifth Avenue, New York, N.Y. 10110
www.wwnorton.com

W. W. Norton & Company Ltd.
Castle House, 75/76 Wells Street, London W1T 3QT

1 2 3 4 5 6 7 8 9 0

For Katherine

Contents

Author's Note   ix

ACT ONE: WAKING

My Dinner with Ali   3

A Boyhood Dream   30

Easter Sunday   32

Interlude: Kuwait   34

Mouse Meets Muhammad Ali   35

ACT TWO: ALL THINGS VIBRATE

Last Apple   57

Ali Offers Vocational Advice   69

The Zen of Muhammad Ali: Part One   89

Interlude: Desert Storm   108

The Zen of Muhammad Ali: Part Two   109

Interlude: Jann Wenner   128

Tokyo   131

Columbus, Ohio   135

The Reverend Doesn't Play Fair . . .   137

And Neither Does His God   139

A Midafternoon Dream   140

All Things Vibrate   142

Of All Times   151

Manila   154

Twenty-Dollar Bills   158

Eleven Ghosts   162

Interlude: Marrakech   177

ACT THREE: A HYMN FOR AGNOSTICS

There Is Nothing in the Universe That You Are Not   183

Tonight's Dream   189

Our Dinner with Ali   194

Sam and Isaac   200

Lonnie   207

From Adam Until Now   208

Acknowledgments   211

Author's Note

*This hour I tell things in confidence I might
not tell everybody, but I will tell you.*
—WALT WHITMAN

IN LATE 1993, AS MUHAMMAD ALI and I sat side by
side on the thick stone wall that framed the driveway of his Berrien
Springs, Michigan, home, he turned to me and said, "I don't talk
much, that's not my way no more. But you're wise, serious; I feel it
rumblin' around inside you. You make me think, and talk." Propped
up high on hunks of sandstone beside Ali, although I didn't consider
myself wise (and now, at sixty-three, I damned well know I'm not),
I felt my entire body swell with pride. And as I'm sitting here at my
keyboard in September 2015, pummeled *and* heartened by the places
the past quarter century of writerly misadventures have taken me, I
still regard his as the greatest compliment anyone has given me.

My history with Ali is long and varied. Ever since I first saw him
in early 1964, when I was a sickly eleven-year-old paralyzed with
sorrow over my mother's recent, unexpected, and inexplicable death,
I've felt a profound, nearly intrinsic connection with The Champ.

In the late 1960s, as a puny, almost catatonic teen living vicariously through Ali, my admiration for him saved my life. In my twenties, inspired by Ali, I became a fine, empowered athlete. In my thirties, struggling to tough out a living as a video store clerk, my developing friendship with him allowed me to finally realize my decades-long dream: with Ali as muse and mentor, I became a writer: a magazine journalist and memoirist, and eventually a book author. Other than my own parents, wives, and children, for over fifty years and in many ways, Ali has been the most reliably large planet in my solar system, the astronomical constant, my friend and great subject.

The primary focus of *Approaching Ali* is not, however, on the numerous ways that Ali has transformed, enlarged, and enriched my world; it is on Ali himself. More specifically, *Approaching Ali* is about the older Ali, who has carried himself with very great dignity through his afflicted middle and late life. The amount of time that Ali has had Parkinson's disease is unprecedented: forty years—more than half of his life. (Although he was first diagnosed in 1984, he has been symptomatic ever since his devastating, life- and body-changing October 1975 fight with Joe Frazier.)

This book is not yet another attempt by an author to define Ali. I've seldom admired from-a-distance biographies; to me, such work feels, in one sense or another, reductive and industrial. In this book, as in all of my Ali stories that preceded it, I will not deconstruct, trivialize, deify, or demonize my multi-lived, many-hearted, con-founding, irrepressible, fantastic, and finally undefinable friend. My task is about exploring and sharing. Ever since I first became friends with Ali, I have looked at him as if I've always known him, and as if I am seeing him for the first time. I believe that this is an interesting perspective to bring to these stories. *Approaching Ali* is a literary telling of my time spent in the company of a great man. Another way of saying it: *Approaching Ali* is a series of nuanced sketches of a friendship; it's in the nuances, the particulars, that a larger truth resides.

Collectively, the pages of *Approaching Ali* comprise what I believe to be the all-time most intimate and quietly startling portrait of Ali's day-by-day life, as well as the only finely detailed look at his enormously rich years after boxing and with Parkinson's. For me, each moment I have spent with Ali is a rounded stone lying true at the bottom of a clean, clear-moving stream. Every stone lives and shines, each in its place. One very intentional result of recounting my Ali stories: I hope that each and every person who reads *Approaching Ali* will come away feeling that they have spent serious time in the company of this singular and extraordinary man.

For more than half a century now, I have been approaching Ali. I handwrote the earliest chapters of this book in 1978, '79, and '80 on Nifty notebook paper and revised them on the Royal manual typewriter my mother used in secretarial school in the late 1940s; I drafted the most recent pages in 2013, '14, and '15 on a Samsung tablet, then spirited them over to my own email addresses, where I revised them.

Some of these stories have been published in shorter forms in my first book, many have never before been shared with readers, many I've written over the past few months, and several were originally published in other, lesser forms in magazines, newspapers, and anthologies in the United States, England, Ireland, Australia, Japan, South Africa, Brazil, and Germany. Over a two-year period, from 2013 to the present, I broadly and deeply rewrote each chapter that had been previously published. I wanted and needed to open up and dig down deep inside each story (every page, each paragraph, each and every sentence); I needed to revise and expand and struggle toward the wisdom that Ali claimed was "rumblin' around" inside me, to toil toward something that would feel true to me now, in my early sixties.

I hope that you'll enjoy *Approaching Ali*, which is the book I've been striving to write ever since I first became friends with Ali in the late 1980s, and which I believe is my best work to date.

I am human, and nothing human is foreign to me.

—TERENCE

Act One

——

WAKING

My Dinner with Ali

One
MARCH 31, 1988

I'D BEEN WAITING FOR YEARS. When it finally happened, it wasn't what I'd expected. But he's been fooling many of us for most of our lives.

When I finally got to see him, it wasn't at his farm in Michigan and I didn't have an appointment. I simply drove past his mother's house on Lambert Avenue in Louisville.

It was midafternoon on Good Friday, two days before Resurrection Day. A block-long ivory-colored Winnebago with Virginia plates was parked out front. Though he hadn't been in town much lately, I knew it was his.

How was I sure? Because I knew his patterns and style. Since 1962, when he has traveled unhurried in this country, he's preferred buses or recreational vehicles. And he owned a second farm in Virginia. The connections were obvious. Some people study faults in the earth's crust or the habits of storms or of galaxies, hoping to make sense of the universe, of the world we live in, and of their own lives. Others meditate on the life and work of one social movement or man. Since I was eleven years old, I have been a Muhammad Ali scholar.

I parked my car behind his Winnebago and grabbed a few old magazines and a special stack of papers I'd been storing under the front seat, waiting for the meeting with Ali that, ever since my family and I'd moved to Louisville two years before, I'd been certain would come. Like everyone else, I wondered in what shape I'd find The Champ. I'd heard about his Parkinson's disease and watched him stumble through the ropes when introduced at recent big fights. But when I thought of Ali, I remembered him as I'd seen him years before, when he was luminous.

I was in my early twenties then, hoping to become a world-champion kickboxer. And I was fortunate enough to get to spar with him. I later wrote a couple of stories about the experience, the ones I had with me today hoping that he'd sign.

Yes, in those days he had shone. There was an aura of light and confidence around him. He had told the world of his importance: "I am the center of the universe," he howled throughout the mid-1970s, and we almost believed him. But recent magazine and newspaper articles had Ali sounding like a turtle spilled on to his back, limbs thrashing air.

It was his brother Rahaman who opened the door. He saw what I was holding under my arm, smiled an understanding smile, and said, "He's out in the Winnebago. Go knock on the door. He'll be happy to sign those for you."

Rahaman looked pretty much the way I remembered him: tall as his brother, mahogany skin, and a mustache that suggested a cross between footballer Jim Brown and a black, aging Errol Flynn. There was no indication in his voice or on his face that I would find his brother less than healthy.

I crossed the yard, climbed the three steps on the side of the Winnebago, and prepared to knock. Ali opened the door before I got the chance. I'd forgotten how huge he was. His presence filled the doorway. He had to lean under the frame to see me.

I felt no nervousness. Ali's face, in many ways, was as familiar to me as my father's. His skin remained unmarked, his countenance had nearly perfect symmetry. Yet something was different: Ali was no longer the world's prettiest man. This was only partly related to his illness; it was also because he was heavier than he needed to be. He remained handsome, even uncommonly so, but in the way of a youngish granddad who tells stories about how he could have been a movie star, if he'd wanted. Ali's pulchritude used to challenge us; now he looked a bit more like us, and less like an avatar sent by Allah.

"Come on in," he said and waved me past. His voice had a gurgle to it, as if he needed to clear his throat. He offered a massive hand. He did not so much shake hands as he lightly placed his in mine. His touch was as gentle as a girl's. His palm was cool and not callused; his fingers were the long, tapered digits of a hypnotist; his fingernails were professionally manicured; his knuckles were large and slightly swollen, as if he recently had been punching the heavy bag.

He was dressed in white, all white: new leather tennis shoes, over-the-calf cotton socks, custom-tailored linen slacks, thick short-sleeved safari-style shirt crisp with starch. I told him I thought white was a better color for him than the black he often wore those days.

He motioned for me to sit, but didn't speak. His mouth was tense at the corners; it looked like a kid's who has been forced by a parent or teacher to keep it closed. He slowly lowered himself into a chair beside the window. I took a seat across from him and laid my magazines on the table between us. He immediately picked them up, produced a pen, and began signing. He asked, "What's your name?" and I told him.

He continued to write without looking up. His eyes were not glazed, as I'd read, but they looked tired. A wet cough rattled in his throat. His left hand trembled almost continuously. In the silence around us, I felt a need to tell him some of the things I'd been wanting to say for years.

"Champ, you changed my life," I said. It's true. "When I was a kid, I was messed up, couldn't even talk to people. No kind of life at all."

He raised his eyes from an old healthy image of himself on a magazine cover. "You made me believe I could do anything," I said.

He was watching me while I talked, not judging, just watching. I picked up a magazine from the stack in front of him. "This is a story I wrote for *Sports Illustrated* when I was in college," I said. "It's about the ways you've influenced my life."

"What's your name?" he asked again, this time looking right at me. I told him. He nodded. "I'll finish signing these in a while," he said. He put his pen on the table. "Read me your story."

✦   ✦   ✦   ✦

"YOU HAVE a good face," he said when I was through. "I like your face. Kind."

He'd listened seriously as I'd read, laughing at funny lines and when I'd tried to imitate his voice. He had not looked bored. It was a lot more than I could have expected.

"You ever seen any magic?" he asked. "You like magic?"

"Not in years," I said.

He stood and walked to the back of his RV, moving mechanically. It was my great-grandfather's walk. He motioned for me to follow. There was a sad yet lovely, noble, and intimate quality to his movements.

He did about ten tricks. The one that interested me most required no props. It was a very simple deception. "Watch my feet," he said, standing maybe eight feet away, his back to me and his arms perpendicular to his sides. Then, although he'd just had real trouble walking, he seemed to levitate about three inches off of the floor. He turned to me and in his thick, slow voice said, "I'm a *baadd* niggah," and gave me the classic easy Ali smile.

I laughed and asked him to do it again; it was a good one. I thought I might like to try it myself, just as fifteen years earlier I had stood in front of the mirror in my dad's hallway for hours, pushing my tapeworm of a left arm out at the reflection, wishing mightily that I could replicate Ali's cobra jab. And I had found an old white cotton laundry bag, filled it with socks and rags, and hung it from a ceiling beam in the basement. I pulled on a pair of my dad's old brown cotton work gloves and pushed my left hand into that twenty-pound marshmallow two hundred, three hundred, five hundred, one thousand times a day—concentrating on speed: dazzling, crackling speed, in pursuit of godly speed, trying to whip out punches so fast they'd be invisible to opponents. I got to where I could shoot six to eight crisp shots a second—"shoe shinin'," Ali called it—and I strove to make my fists move more quickly than thought (like Ali's); and then I'd try to spring up on my toes, as I had watched Ali do: I would try to fly like Ali, bounding away from the bag and to my left.

After the levitation trick, Ali grabbed an empty plastic milk jug from beside a sink. He asked me to examine it. "What if I make this jug rise up from the sink this high and sit there? Will you believe?"

"Not much of a believer these days, Champ," I said.

"Well, what if I make it rise, sit this high off the ground, then turn in a circle?"

"I'm a hard man to convince," I said.

"Well, what if I make it rise, float over here to the other side of the room, then go back to the sink, and sit itself back down. Then will you become . . . one of my believers?"

I laughed and said, "Then I'll believe."

"Watch," he said, pointing at the plastic container and taking four steps back. I was trying to see both the milk jug and Ali. He waved his hands a couple of times in front of his body, said, "Arise, ghost, arise," in a foggy-sounding voice. The plastic container did not move from the counter.

"April Fool's," said Ali. We both chuckled and he walked over and slipped his long arm around my shoulders.

✦   ✦   ✦   ✦

HE AUTOGRAPHED the stories and wrote a note on a page of my book-length manuscript I'd asked him to take a look at. "To Davis Miller, The Greatest Fan of All Times," he wrote. "From Muhammad Ali, King of Boxing."

I felt my stories were finally complete, now that he'd confirmed their existence. He handed me the magazines and asked me into his mother's house. We left the Winnebago. I unlocked my car and leaned across the front seat, carefully placing the magazines and manuscript on the passenger's side, not wanting to take a chance of damaging them or leaving them behind. Abruptly, there was a chirping, insect-sounding noise in my ear. I jumped back, swatted the air, turned around. It had been Ali's hand. He was standing right behind me, still the practical joker.

"How'd you do that?" I wanted to know. It was a question I'd find myself asking several times that day.

He didn't answer. Instead, he raised both fists to shoulder height and motioned me out into the yard. We walked about five paces, I put up my hands, and he tossed a slow jab at me. I blocked and countered with my own. Many fighters throw punches at each other or at the air or at whatever happens to be around. It's the way we play, even decades after having last stepped between the ropes of a prize ring. Now, approaching ten years after his retirement, Ali must still have tossed a hundred lefts a day. He and I had both thrown our shots a full half foot away from the other, but my adrenal gland was pumping at high gear from being around Ali and my jab had come out fast—it had made the air sing. He slid back a half step and took a serious look at me. I figured I was going to get it now. A couple of kids were riding past on bicycles; they recognized Ali and stopped.

"He doesn't understand I'm the greatest boxer of all times," he yelled to the kids. He pulled his watch from his arm, stuck it in his pants pocket. I slipped mine off, too. He'd get down to business now. He got up on his skates, danced to his left a little, loosening his legs. A couple of minutes before, climbing down the steps of his RV, he'd moved so awkwardly he'd almost lost his balance. I'd wanted to give him a hand, but knew not to. I'd remembered seeing old Joe Louis "escorted" in that fashion by lesser mortals, and I couldn't do that to Muhammad Ali. But now that Ali was on his toes and boxing, he was moving fairly fluidly.

He flung another jab in my direction, a second, a third. He wasn't one-fourth as fast as he had been in 1975, when I'd sparred with him, but his eyes were alert, shining like black electric marbles, and he saw everything and was real relaxed. That's one reason old fighters keep making comebacks: we are more alive when boxing than at almost any other time. The grass around us was green and was getting high; it would soon need its first cutting. A blue jay squawked from a big oak to the left. Six robins roamed the yard. The afternoon light was tawny. New leaves looked wet with the sun. I instinctively blocked and/or slid to the side of all three of Ali's punches, then immediately felt guilty about it, like being fourteen years old and knowing for the first time that you can beat your dad at ping-pong. I wished I could've stopped myself from slipping Ali's jabs, but I couldn't. Reflexive training runs faster and deeper than thought. I zipped a jab to his nose, one to his body, vaulted a straight right up to his chin, and was dead certain all three would have scored—and scored clean. A couple of cars stopped in front of the house. His mom's was on a corner lot. Three more were parked on the side.

"Check out the left," a young-sounding voice said from somewhere. The owner of the voice was talking about my jab, not Ali's.

"He's in with the triple greatest of all times," Ali was shouting. "Gowna let him tire himself out. He'll get tired soon."

I didn't, but pretended to, anyway. "You're right, Champ," I told him, dropping my hands to my sides. "I'm thirty-five. Can't go like I used to."

I raised my right hand to my chest, acting out of breath. I looked at Ali; his hand was in the exact same position. We were both smiling, but he was sizing me up.

"He got scared," Ali shouted, conclusively.

Onlookers laughed from their bicycles and car windows. Someone blew his horn and another yelled, "Hey, Champ."

"Come on in the house," Ali said softly in my ear.

We walked toward the door, Ali in the lead, moving woodenly through new grass, while all around us people rolled up car windows and started their engines.

Two

"**GOWNA MOVE BACK TO LOOVUL,** just part time."

The deep Southern melody rolled sleepily in Ali's voice. His words came scarcely louder than whisper and were followed by a short fit of coughing.

Back to Loovul. Back to hazy orange sunsets and ancestors' unmarked graves; back to old slow-walking family (real and acquired), empty sidewalks, nearly equatorial humidity, and to peach cobblers made by heavy, round-breasted aunts wearing flowered dresses; back to short thin uncles and their straw hats, white open-collared shirts, black shiny pants, and spit-shined black Florsheims—back to a life that hadn't been Ali's since he was eighteen years old.

We were standing in the "family room," a space so dark I could not imagine the drapes ever having been drawn, a room furnished with dented gold-painted furniture, filled with smells of cooking meat, and infused with a light not dissimilar to that from a fireplace fire.

Ali had introduced me to his mother, Mrs. Odessa Grady Clay, and to Rahaman, then suddenly he was gone.

Ali's family easily accepted me. They were not surprised to have a visitor and handled me with ritualistic charm and grace. Rahaman told me to make myself at home, offered a root beer, went to get it.

I took a seat on the sofa beside Ali's mother. Mrs. Clay was in her early seventies, yet her face had few wrinkles. Short, her hair nearly as orange as those Louisville sunsets, she was freckled, fragile-looking and pretty. Ali's face is shaped much like his mother's. During all the years he was fighting, she was quite heavy, but she had lost what looked to be about seventy-five pounds over the past ten years.

Mrs. Clay was watching Oprah Winfrey on a big old wooden floor-model TV. I was wondering where Ali had gone. Rahaman brought the drink, a paper napkin, and a coaster. Mrs. Clay patted me on the hand. "Don't worry," she said. "Ali hasn't left you. I'm sure he's just gone upstairs to say his prayers."

I hadn't realized that my anxiety was showing. But Ali's mother had watched him bring home puppies many times during his forty-six years. "He's always been a restless man, like his daddy," she said. "Can't ever sit still."

Mrs. Clay spoke carefully, with a mother's sweet sadness about her. The dignified clip to her voice must once have seemed affected, but after cometing all over the globe with Ali, it now sounded authentically old-money, poised-Kentuckian in its inflections.

"Have you met Lonnie, Ali's new wife?" she asked. "He's known her since she was a baby. I'm so happy for him. She's my best friend's daughter, we used to all travel to his fights together. She's a smart girl, has a master's degree in business. She's so good to him, doesn't use him. He told me, 'Mom, Lonnie's better to me than all the other three put together.' She treats him so good. He needs somebody to take care of him."

Just then, Ali came back to the room, carrying himself high and with stately dignity, though his footing was unsteady. He fell deep into a chair on the other side of the room.

"You tired, baby?" Mrs. Clay asked.

"Tired, I'm always tired," he said, rubbing his face twice and closing his eyes.

He must have felt me watching or was simply conscious of someone other than family being in the room. His eyes weren't closed ten
seconds before he shook himself awake, balled his hands into fists,
and started making typical Ali faces and noises at me—sticking his
teeth out over his lower lip, looking fake-mean, growling, other playful cartoon kid stuff. After a few seconds he asked, "Y-y-you okay?"
He was so difficult to understand that I didn't so much hear him as I
conjectured what he must have been saying. "Y-y-you need anything?
They takin' care of you?" I assured him that I was fine.

He made a loud clucking noise by pressing his tongue across the
roof of his mouth and popping it forward. Rahaman came quickly
from the kitchen. Ali motioned him close and whispered in his ear.
Rahaman went back to the kitchen. Ali turned to me. "Come sit
beside me," he said, patting a bar stool to his right. He waited for me
to take my place, then said, "You had any dinner? Sit and eat with me."

"Can I use the phone? I need to call home and let my wife know."

"You got kids?" he asked. I told him I had two. He asked how old.
I told him the ages.

"They know me?" he asked.

"Even the two-year-old. He throws punches at the TV whenever
I play your fights."

He nodded, satisfied. "Bring 'em over Sunday," he said, matter-of-
factly. "I'll do my magic for 'em. Here's my mother's number. Be sure
to phone first."

I called Lyn and told her where I was and what I was doing. She
didn't seem surprised. She asked me to pick up a gallon of milk on
the way home. I was sure she was excited for me, but we had a lot
of history, some of it rough, and she wouldn't show emotion in her
voice simply because I was hanging out with my childhood idol. In

September 1977, near the beginning of our first semester at East
Carolina University, I packed my car with clothes for Lyn and me,
picked her up from her noon art class, and drove straight to the
bank, where we withdrew all of the money our parents had given us
for the semester.

"Terry, sorry I'm not in class today," began the note I left on my
writing teacher's office door. "I've taken my girlfriend to New York to
see the Muhammad Ali–Earnie Shavers fight. Oh, we're also going
to get married while we're there. See you next week. Davis."

Lyn and I drove straight through the night, arriving in Manhattan the morning of the bout. Early afternoon, as we checked into
a Howard Johnson's in New Jersey, Lyn put on the wedding band
I'd purchased months before. We then drove from the motel back
into the city, and, at a shop in the Waldorf-Astoria, she bought a
simple jade ring for me. As we were leaving the hotel, we spotted
Ali on the street. Traffic stopped in all directions. Thousands of
us followed him as he walked to Madison Square Garden for the
weigh-in. Even though there were several people near Ali who were
taller and bigger than he, he looked larger than anyone I had seen
in my life. There was a wakeful silence around him. As if his very
skin was listening. There was pushing and shoving near the outside
of the circle of people around Ali. Lyn and I stood on a concrete
wall away from the clamor and looked down on him. There was a
softness, a quietude, near the center of the circle; those closest to
Ali were gentle and respectful.

That night in the Garden was the first time I'd seen twenty thousand people move as one organism. The air was alive with smells of
pretzels and hot dogs, beer and marijuana. It was Ali's last good fight.
Shavers's longtime ring nickname, "One Punch," had been arrived at
because it took him exactly one good, clean, orgasmic overhand right
to flatten opponents. Although few casual boxing fans had heard of
Shavers, ring insiders regarded his right cross as the hardest of any-

one's in the history of pugilism. Bigger than all of Foreman's punches. Bigger than Frazier's best left hook. Tonight, Ali was regularly hurt by Shavers's rights and would later say that Shavers had hit him harder than anyone ever. So resounding were the shots with which Shavers tagged Ali that Lyn and I heard them, the sound arriving what seemed a full second after we saw the punches connect, as we sat a quarter of a mile up and away from the ring. In round fifteen, we were all suddenly standing and not realizing that we had stood. I was trembling, Lyn was holding my hand, and thousands of us were chanting, *"Ahh-lee, Ahh-lee,"* his name our mantra, as his gloves melded into vermilion lines of tracers and Shavers finally bowed before him.

The next morning, after watching Ali hold forth on the *Today* show and checking out of our motel, Lyn and I drove back to Manhattan to get a marriage license. That's when we discovered that there was a three-day waiting period. We had spent all but forty dollars of our money at the fight, on the motel, and on my wedding band. We could not afford to stay; she was very disappointed. Throughout our long drive back to eastern North Carolina, she stayed mostly silent and hung her head down toward her lap. When she'd started college, I'd known it was the first time she'd been away from her parents' house (the one and only home in which she'd lived) for longer than a weekend. What I hadn't recognized was how unformed she was, how young emotionally. Before the trip she'd seemed so tough; it surprised me that she depended on me even more than I on her. This was the first time she had seen me fail. To this day she's never gotten over it, a fact that initiated an ever-present darkening of our relationship. I was disappointed, too, but remained certain that she would soon cut loose, beyond the pull of gravity; she would become the ballsy, happier, primal-woods creature she really was inside.

The day we returned from New York she moved into my off-campus apartment, and for the rest of the year neither of us was

able to find a job. We had to live off of what little money I was able to make modeling for art classes at the university. Even though I was certain everything would work out well, for Lyn it was a horrible time. I'd come in from classes and find her in tears, worrying about what her parents would do when they found out we'd blown their money and she was living with me. She eventually quit school because she had no funds to buy materials for her art classes. It would be nearly a year before we again felt we could afford to get married. Every weekend, to pay our electric bills, we filled a laundry bag (the same one I'd once used as a boxing bag) with returnable soda bottles we picked up beside highways. But, all these years later, I know that I'd be willing to do it the exact same way to see Ali in one of his last fights.

✦   ✦   ✦   ✦

NOW RAHAMAN brought two large bowls of chili and two enormously thick slices of white bread from the kitchen. Ali and I sat at our chairs, took spoons in our hands. He put his face down close to the bowl and the food was gone. Three minutes, tops. As I continued to eat, he spoke easily to me. "I remember what it was like to meet Joe Louis and Rocky Marciano for the first time," he said. "They were my idols. I'd seen their fights and faces so many times I felt I knew them. Want to treat you right, don't want to disappoint you.

"Do you know how many people in the world would like to have the opportunity you're getting, how many would like to come into my house and spend the day with me?" he said. "Haven't fought in seven years and still get over four hundred letters a week."

I asked how people got his address.

He looked puzzled. "I don't know," he answered, shaking his head. "Sometimes they come addressed 'Muhammad Ali, Los Angeles,

California, USA.' Don't have a house in L.A. no more, but the letters still get to me.

"I want to get me a place, a coffee shop, where I can give away free coffee and doughnuts and people can just sit around and talk, people of all races, and I can go and talk to people. Have some of my old robes and trunks and gloves around, show old fight films, call it 'Ali's Place.'"

"I'd call it 'Ali's,'" I said, not believing there would or ever could be such a place but enjoying sharing his dream with him. "Just 'Ali's,' that's enough."

"'Ali's'?" he repeated, and his eyes focused inward, visualizing the dream.

"People would know what it was," I said.

I asked if he had videotapes of his fights. He shook his head no.

"Well, look," I said, "I manage a video store."

"You're rich," he said, pointing and chuckling, but also being serious.

"No, no, I'm not. I just try to make a living. Look . . . why don't we go to the store and get a tape of your fights, and we can watch it tonight. Would you like that? You want to ride with me?"

"I'll drive," Ali said.

✦   ✦   ✦   ✦

There was a rubber monster mask in the Winnebago that I wore on my hand on the way to the store, pressing it against the window at stoplights. A couple of times, people in cars saw the mask, then recognized Ali. Ali wore glasses when he read and when he drove. Every time that he saw someone looking at him, he carefully removed his glasses, placed them in his lap, made his hands into fists, and put them up beside his head.

Other than my alcoholic grandfather near the end of his life, Ali was the worst driver I'd ever ridden with. He careened from lane to lane, sometimes riding down the middle of the highway, and he often switched lanes without looking or giving turn signals. Still wearing the monster mask on my right hand, I balled my fists in my lap and pretended to be relaxed. A group of teenage boys became infuriated when he cut them off in their beat-up and rusted-out 1970s Firebird. Three of them leaned out the windows, shooting him the finger. Ali shot it back.

When we made it to the store, my co-workers acted as if they'd been stricken dumb. Instead of doing what they always did— talking about the day's business or problems they were having with customers or other employees, they stayed away and simply stared at Ali. We borrowed an early-1970s Godzilla movie Ali wanted to see and a tape of his fights and interviews called *Ali: Skill, Brains and Guts* that was written and directed by Jimmy Jacobs, the international handball champion and fight historian. Jacobs had recently died of a degenerative illness. Ali hadn't known of Jacobs's death until I told him.

"He was a good man," Ali said. His voice had that same quality that an older person's takes on who daily reads obituaries. "Did you know Bundini died?" he asked, speaking in the same tone he'd use with a friend of many years. I felt honored by his intimacy and told him that I'd heard.

In the Winnebago on the way back to his mom's, he said, "You're sincere. After thirty years, I can tell."

"I know a lot of people have tried to use you," I said.

"They *have* used me. But it don't matter. I don't let it change me."

I stopped by my car again on the way into Mrs. Clay's house. There was one more picture I hoped Ali would sign, but earlier I'd felt I might be imposing on him. It was a classic head shot in a beautiful out-of-print biography by Wilfrid Sheed that featured hundreds of wonderfully reproduced color plates. I grabbed the book from the car and followed Ali into the house.

When we were seated, I handed him the book and he signed the picture on the title page. "To Davis Miller, From Muhammad Ali, King of Boxing," he wrote, "3-31-88." And then, on the opposite page, which bore only his name in bold block lettering, he inscribed, "After me, there will never be another."

I was about to ask if he'd mind autographing the photo I especially wanted, but he turned to page three, signed that picture, then the next page and the next. He continued to sign for probably forty-five minutes, writing comments about opponents ("Get up Chump," he wrote beside the classic photo of the fallen Sonny Liston), parents, Elijah Muhammad ("The man who named me"), Howard Cosell ("Crazy"), spouses ("She gave me Hell," he scrawled across his first wife's picture; "Love is the net where Hearts are Caught like Fish," he carefully inscribed on a photo of him with his gleaming future wife, then seventeen-year-old Belinda Boyd, in her father's South Side Chicago bakery), then passed the book to his mother and brother to autograph a family portrait. He even signed "Cassius Clay" on several photos from the early sixties. He flipped twice through the book, autographing dozens and dozens of photos, pointing out annotations as he wrote.

"Never done this before," he said. "Usually sign one or two pictures."

As he turned from page to page, he stopped and studied, then autographed, a picture of his youthful self with the Louisville Sponsoring Group, the collective of rich white businessmen who owned his contract (and reputedly those of several race horses) until he became Muslim. He also hesitated over a famous posed shot taken for *Life* magazine in 1963, in a bank vault. In this photo, a wide-eyed and beaming Cassius Clay sits atop one million one-dollar bills. Ali turned to me and said, "Money don't mean nothin'," signed the picture with his childhood name, and leafed to a picture with Malcolm X, which he autographed, then posed his pen above the signature, as if prepared to make another annotation. Suddenly, though, he closed the book, looked at me dead level, and held it out at arms' length with both hands. "I'm giving you somethin' very valuable," he said, handing me the biography as if deeding me the book of life.

I stared at the book in my open palms and felt I should say something, should thank him in some way. I carefully placed it on a table, shook my head slightly, and cleared my throat, but found no words.

Three

I EXCUSED MYSELF to the bathroom, locking the door behind me. A pair of Ali's huge, shiny-black, businessman's dress shoes was on the floor beside the toilet. The toe of one had been crushed, the other was lying on its side. When I unlocked the door to leave, it wouldn't budge. I couldn't even turn the handle. After trying several times, I tentatively knocked. There was laughter from the other room. I distinctly heard Mrs. Clay and Rahaman murmuring. I yanked fairly hard on the door a few times. Nothing. Just when I was beginning to think I was stuck in Odessa Clay's bathroom for the millennium, the door easily opened. I caught a glimpse of Ali bounding into a side room to the right, laughing and high-stepping like some oversized, out-of-shape Nubian leprechaun.

I peeked around the corner. He was standing with his back flat against the wall. He saw me, jumped from the room, and tickled me, a guilty-little-kid smile splashed across his features. Next thing I knew, he had me on the floor, balled up in a fetal position, tears flowing down both sides of my face, laughing. Then he stopped tickling me and helped me to my feet. Everybody kept laughing. Mrs. Clay's face was round and wide with laughter. One-fourth Irish, her ancestry traceable to the village of Ennis, County Clare, the former Odessa Grady looked like the mom of a Celtic imp.

"What'd you think happened to the door?" Rahaman asked. I told him I'd figured it was Ali. "Then why you turnin' red?" he wanted to know.

"It's not every day," I said, "that I go to Muhammad Ali's, he locks me in the bathroom, then tickles me into submission."

Everyone laughed again. "Ali, you crazy," Rahaman said.

Suddenly, I recognized the obvious: that all afternoon I'd been acting like a teenage admirer again. And that Muhammad Ali had not lost perhaps his most significant talent—the ability to transport people past thoughts and words to a world of feeling and play. Being around Ali, or watching him perform on TV, has always made me feel genuinely childlike. I looked at his family: they were beaming. Ali still flipped their switches, too.

After helping me up, he trudged off to the bathroom. Rahaman crept over from his seat on the sofa and held the door, trying to keep Ali in. The brothers pushed and tugged on the door and, when Ali got out, laughed and wrestled around the room. Then Ali threw several feathery punches at Rahaman and a few at me.

We finally slipped the Ali tape into the VCR. Rahaman brought everyone another root beer and we settled back to watch, he to my left, Ali beside me on the right, and Mrs. Clay beside Ali. The family's reactions to the tape were not unlike those you or I would have, looking at old home movies or the photos in high school yearbooks. Everyone sighed and their mouths arced at tender angles. "Oh, look at Bundini," Mrs. Clay said. "Hey, there's Otis," Rahaman offered.

When there was footage of Ali reciting verse, everyone recited with him. "Those were the days," Rahaman said several times, to which Mrs. Clay responded, "Yes, yes, they were," in a slow, lamenting lilt.

After a half hour or so, she left the room. Rahaman continued to watch the tape for a while, pointing out people and events, but then said he was going to bed. He brought a pen and piece of paper. "Give your name and number," he said, smiling. "We'll look you up."

Then it was just Ali and me. On the TV, it was early 1964 and he was framed on the left by Jim Jacobs and on the right by Drew "Bundini" Brown. "They both dead now," he said, an acute awareness of his own mortality in the tone.

For a time, he continued to stare at the old Ali on the screen, but eventually he lost interest in peering at the distant mountains of his youth. "Did my mom go upstairs? Do you know?" he asked, his voice carrying no further than mine would if I had a hand over my mouth.

"Yeah, I think she's probably asleep."

He nodded, stood, and left the room, presumably to check on her. When he came back, he was moving heavily. His shoulder hit the frame of the door to the kitchen. He went in and came out with two fistfuls of cookies, crumbs all over his mouth. He sat beside me on the sofa. Our knees were touching. Usually, when a man gets this close, I instinctively pull away. He offered a couple of cookies, yawned a giant's yawn, closed his eyes, and seemed to go dead asleep.

"Champ, you want me to leave?" I said. "Am I keeping you up?"

He slowly opened his eyes and was back to our side of The Great Mystery. The pores on his face looked huge, his features elongated, distorted, like someone's in an El Greco. He rubbed his face the way I rub mine when I haven't shaved in a week.

"No, stay," he said. His tone was very gentle.

"You'd let me know if I was staying too late?"

He hesitated only slightly before he answered. "I go to bed at eleven," he said.

With the volume turned this low on the TV, you could hear the videotape's steady whir.

"Can I ask a serious question?" I said. He nodded okay.

"You're still a great man, Champ, I see that. But a lot of people think your mind is fried. Does that bother you?"

He didn't hesitate before answering. "No, there are ignorant people everywhere," he said. "Even educated people can be ignorant."

"Does it bother you that you're a great man not being allowed to be great?"

"Wh-wh-whatcha you mean, 'not allowed to be great'?" he said, his voice hardly finding its way out of his body.

"I mean . . . let me think about what I mean . . . I mean the things you seem to care most about, the things you enjoy doing best, the things the rest of us think of as *being* Muhammad Ali, those are precisely the things that have been taken from you. It just doesn't seem fair."

"You don't question God," he said, his voice rattling in his throat.

"Okay, I respect that, but . . . aw, man, I don't have any business talking to you about this."

"No, no, go on," he said.

"It just bothers me," I told him. I was thinking about the obvious ironies, thinking about Ali continuing to invent, and be invented by, his own mythology. About how he used to talk more easily, and more relentlessly, than anybody in the world (has anyone in history so enjoyed the sweet and spiky melodies of his own voice?); about how he still thought with speed and dazzle, but it took serious effort for him to communicate even with people close to him, including his own mother. About how he may have been the world's best athlete— when walking, he used to move with the mesmeric grace of a leopard turning a corner; now, at night, he stumbled around the house. About how it was his left hand, the same hand from which once slid that great singular Ali snake lick of a jab—the most visible phenomenon of his boxing greatness—the very hand with which he won more than 150 sanctioned fights and tens of thousands of sparring sessions, it's *his left hand*, not his right, that shook almost continuously.

And I was thinking how his major source of pride, his "prettiness," remained more or less intact. If Ali lost forty pounds, in the right kind of light, he'd still look classically Greek. The seeming precision with which things have been excised from Ali's life, as well as the gifts that have been left him, sort of spooked me.

"I know why this has happened," Ali said. "God is showing me, and showing *you*"—he pointed his shaking index finger at me and widened his eyes—"that I'm just a man, just like everybody else."

We sat a long quiet time then, and watched his flickering image on the television screen. It's now 1971 and there was footage of him training for the first Frazier fight. Our Most Public Figure was then The World's Most Beautiful Man and The Greatest Athlete of All Time, his copper skin glowing under the fluorescents, secret rhythms springing in loose firmness from his fingertips.

"Champ, I think it's time for me to go," I said again and made an effort to stand.

"No, stay. You my man," he says, patting my leg. He has always been this way, always wanted to be around people. I take his accolade as one of the greatest compliments of my life.

"I'll tell you a secret," he says, leaning close. "I'm gowna make a comeback."

"What?" I say. I think he's joking, hope he is, but something in his tone makes me uncertain. "You're not serious?" I ask.

And suddenly there is power in his voice. "I'm gowna make a comeback," he repeats louder, more firmly.

"Are you serious?"

"The timing is perfect. They'd think it was a miracle, wouldn't they?" He's speaking distinctly, crisply; he's easy to understand. It's almost the voice I remember from when I first met him in 1975, the one that seemed to come roiling up from down in his belly. In short, Ali sounds like Ali.

"Wouldn't they?" he asks again.

"It *would* be a miracle," I say.

"Nobody'll take me serious at first. But then I'll get my weight down to two-fifteen and have an exhibition at Yankee Stadium or someplace. Then they'll believe. I'll fight for the title. It'll be bigger than the Resurrection." He stands and walks to the center of the room.

"It'd be good to get your weight down," I say.

"Watch this," he says and dances to his left, studying himself in the mirror above the TV. His new, clean, bright white shoes bound around the carpet; I marvel at how easily he moves. His white clothing accentuates his movements in the dark room; the white appears to make him glow. He starts throwing punches—not the kind he'd tossed at me earlier, but now really letting them go. I'd thought what he'd thrown in the yard was indicative of what he had left. But what he'd done was allow me to play; he'd wanted me to enjoy myself.

"Look at the TV. That's 1971 and I'm just as fast now." One second, two seconds, twelve punches flash in the night. This can't be real. Yet it is. The old man can still do it: he can still make fire appear in the air. He looks faster standing in front of me than do the ghost-like Ali images on the screen. God, I wish I had a video camera to tape this. Nobody would believe me.

"And I'll be even faster when I get my weight down," he tells me.

"You know more now, too," I find myself admitting. Jesus, what am I saying? And why am I saying this? This is a sick man.

"Do you believe?" he asks.

"Well . . . ," I say. *God, the Parkinson's is affecting his sanity. Look at the gray shining in his hair. The guy can hardly walk, for Christ's sake.* Just because he was my boyhood idol doesn't mean I'm blinded to what his life is now like.

And Ali throws another three dozen blows at the gods of mortality, the variety of punches as unpredictable and mesmerizing as starling murmurations. He springs a *triple* hook off of a jab, each punch so quick it trails lines of light, drops straight right leads faster than (most fighters') jabs, erupts into a storm of uppercuts, and the air pops, and his fists and feet whir. This is his best work. His highest art. The very combinations no one has ever thrown quite like Muhammad Ali. When he was fighting, he typically held back some; this is the stuff he seldom *had* to use.

"Do you believe?" he asks, breathing hard.

"They wouldn't let you, even if you could do it," I say, thinking, *There's so much concern everywhere for your health. Everybody thinks they see old Mr. Thanatos waiting for you.*

"Do you *believe*?" he asks again.

"I believe," I hear myself say.

He stops dancing and points a magician's finger at me. Then I get the look, the smile that has closed one hundred thousand interviews.

"April Fool's," he says, sitting down hard beside me again. His mouth is hanging open and his breathing sounds raw. The smell of sweat comes from his skin.

We sit in silence for several minutes. I look at my watch. It's eleven-eighteen. I hadn't realized it was that late. I'd told Lyn I'd be in by eight.

"Champ, I better go home. I have a wife and kids waiting."

"Okay," he says almost inaudibly, looking into the distance, not thinking about me anymore, yawning the kind of long uncovered yawn people usually do among family.

He's bone-tired. I'm tired, too, but I want to leave by saying something that will mean something to him, something that will set me apart from the two billion other people he's met, that will imprint me indelibly in his memory and make the kind of impact on his life that he has made on mine. I want to say the words that will cure his Parkinson's.

Instead I say, "See you Easter, Champ."

He coughs and gives me his hand. "Be cool and look out for the

ladies." His words are so volumeless and full of fluid that I don't realize what he's said until I'm halfway out the door.

I don't recall picking up the book he signed, but I must have:
it's beside my typewriter now. I can't remember walking across his
mom's yard and don't remember starting the car. But I do recall what
was playing on the tape deck. It was "The Promise of Living" from
the orchestral suite to Aaron Copland's *The Tender Land*.

✦   ✦   ✦   ✦

I DON'T FORGET Lyn's gallon of milk. Doors to the grocery store
whoosh closed behind me. For this time of night, there are quite
a few customers in the store. They seem to move more as floating
shadows than as people.

An old feeling comes across me that I almost immediately recognize. The sensation is much like going out into the day-to-day world
after making love for the first ever time. It's that same sense of having landed in a lesser reality. And of having a secret that the rest of
the world can't see.

I reach to grab a milk jug and catch my reflection in the chrome
of the dairy counter. There's a half smile on my face and I hadn't
realized it.

"Love is the net where Hearts are Caught like Fish."

A Boyhood
Dream

I'M BACK AT MOUNT TABOR High School. In the hall outside the door marked PRINCIPAL. Middle-aged now, but here I am, still a student. I've had to go back, to make up for all time uselessly spent.

Mike S. is standing in front of me, blowing Winston cigarette smoke in my face. Mike G. is over beside him, waiting for me to walk past so he can yank hard on my necktie and strangle me. Mike J. and Tim S. are both sneering at me the same way they always do, as if my simple existence is beneath any other reaction. And smirking Mike M. is slouching against a wall beside a kid I'll call Mike H., maybe the dumbest kid in school. Mike H. had a bevy of girlfriends, most of whom looked almost exactly alike. When you passed him in the halls, he was often dragging one of their giant-breasted bodies around by its long, thin blond hair. Mike H., Mount Tabor's premier athlete, who spent every other weekend in county jail for having been caught (time and again) driving with a revoked license, who spelled Tabor with an *e* instead of an *o*, and who was always calling *me* stupid.

"Look at that stupid Jewnigger hair," he'd spit in spasms, or "that stupid Jewboy nose." And he'd laugh, sticking a couple of short, thick fingers onto the sides of my nose and giving the cartilage a not-playful twist.

They're all here, and they're still seventeen. I'm in the middle of a circle they've formed around me. They move for me as one.

I slide toward Mike H. first, slip under his overhand right, and bolo-punch his thick, slow body into the wall ten feet away. The blow flows out from the center of my abdomen, is explosive, and the moment of contact with his chin goes good and warm from my fingers, up and across and into my chest. I step outside their circle, fully ready to whup 'em all. But from the principal's office steps . . . Muhammad Ali! White-on-black pinstripe suit, red silk tie, shining black street dogs, glowing cinnamon-colored skin. Captain Clean, as usual. His hands are as large as paddles. His feet blur into the Ali shuffle. And then he slaps all my enemies for me, needing only one effortless, quarter-hard, quarter-speed blow for each of these jerks.

"Thanks, Champ," I say. He smiles his easy Ali smile and steps back through the office door. I know the perfect way to repay his kindness.

"I'll spank ole Smokin' Joe for you," I say, absolutely confident I can actualize my boast.

Ali's inscription on an earlier version of the
previous chapter, "A Boyhood Dream."

Easter Sunday

APRIL 3, 1988

TAKING ALI AND HIS MOM UP ON THEIR OFFER, on Easter Sunday afternoon Lyn and our daughter Johanna and I drive over to Mrs. Clay's. We leave our two-year-old son Isaac with a babysitter, not wanting to risk him breaking something or stressing out Ali's mom.

"You should have brought him along," Mrs. Clay says to Lyn as we take seats in the family room. "He couldn't do anything I haven't seen before. When Ali was a baby, I was changing his diaper. I leaned over and he hit me in the mouth. Knocked out both my front teeth. That's when I knew he was going to be somebody. That's when I knew he was going to be someone special."

Ali stands from his seat on the sofa, walks to Lyn, hugs her (she sheepishly returns his embrace), hugs me, offers Lyn a seat, and then reaches for Johanna, who scurries behind me and clutches the legs of my jeans. I coax her out and Ali picks her up and cradles her to his chest.

His twin daughters, Rasheda and Jamillah, students at the University of Illinois, are in town for the holiday. Ali performs magic for Johanna (who continues to hide behind my jeans legs at every opportunity) and argues with his daughters about their style of dress and makeup.

"Christian men'll be lookin' at you," he says, leaning forward and arching his head with urgency. "You'll get yourselves in trouble."

Do his daughters recognize that their father is speaking as much about the philandering Muhammad Ali of the 1970s as he is about "Christian men"? The girls are tall, lithe, classically beautiful, generally unharmed by the world. And young enough to believe themselves immortal.

"Daddy, you're so old-fashioned," they tell him in stereo. Jamillah punches him on the left biceps, and from the other side Rasheda dismisses him with a peck on the cheek.

We eat lemon pound cake and vanilla ice cream and watch TV. Lyn and Mrs. Clay talk about the season and flower gardens. Lyn promises to paint Ali's mom a vase of violets and buttercups. I ask Ali if he still travels. "All the time," he says. "Just got back from Afghanistan. That's where I was when Bundini died. Flyin' to Kuwait on Tuesday. Be gone a few days."

As Lyn, Johanna, and I prepare to leave, he asks Rahaman to give me the phone number at his farm in Michigan. "Call me," he says. "You my man."

Interlude:
Kuwait

EARLY WEDNESDAY MORNING, *while driving to work, I listen to the news on NPR. Kuwait Airlines Flight 422, on which Ali was a scheduled passenger and guest of the Kuwaiti royal family, has been hijacked. Two people have been murdered and their bodies dumped on the tarmac in Cyprus; the remaining passengers are hostages.*

I pull into an Interstate 64 rest area and call Mrs. Clay's. She answers the phone. "Don't worry," she says of her (and Allah's) son. "He's still here. His trip was canceled yesterday morning."

Mouse Meets Muhammad Ali

This story was written as a nonfiction novel. My personal chronology in the story is less than accurate. The majority of details are true and factual.

One

OCTOBER 1974

MY NAME IS MOUSE. For years I've been smaller than everybody else my age. I'm seventeen years old, four feet, nine inches tall, and I weigh sixty pounds. My pediatrician, Dr. Glenn, says I'll never get much larger.

My size is the reason guys at school call me Mouse. That and the fact I have stand-up-high ears and a small nervous mouth that sits way back behind my too-big nose.

The name my parents gave me isn't Mouse. It's Davis. But I almost never get called by my real name. When guys aren't calling me Mouse or other meaner harder names that aren't me, they're doing other stuff to me. They punch me in the stomach, strip my trousers from my legs and push me into the girls' restrooms, lock my skinny bones up in lockers. Or they drag me out to the courtyard and sit me up on high tree branches they know I'm not strong enough to climb down from. Sometimes they drape me across their shoulders and spin me around and around until my face gets covered with hives and I'm so dizzy I just about throw up. Then they put me on the ground and my hair is standing up on end while the rest of me is lying down. They always laugh when they do these things. I don't want this stuff done to me, but I'm not big enough or fast enough or motivated enough to outrun anybody.

What they don't know is that I have a secret. A big, bad, walloping secret that protects me from everything they do and say. Inside of me, where they can't see, I'm bigger than everyone who bullies me. Inside of me, I'm the biggest and strongest and fastest and greatest man in the world. Inside of me, I'm Muhammad Ali.

✦   ✦   ✦   ✦

OF COURSE, I'm not really Muhammad Ali. He's the king of boxing and the most famous man in the world. And I'm a shriveled little seventeen-year-old mouse at Mount Tabor High School in Winston-Salem, North Carolina. But for months and months I've been looking hard at my life, and today I've made the decision I'm going to become just like Ali. Or at least as much like him as I can, considering the pissant me I'm forced to work with.

I first saw Ali in January 1964. I was seven years old, the shortest, skinniest, and sickliest kid in town. My mother had died that past August from a kidney disease that she and my dad and my sister and me and even our family doctor didn't know she had. After my mom died, I shut myself off from the world. I quit eating and just about stopped talking, answering Daddy and everybody else mostly by grunting. That fall, he had to rush me to Baptist Hospital a couple of times, where doctors and nurses stuck long, fat needles in me and pumped me full of fluids and fed me through tubes because I wouldn't eat or drink anything.

When I wasn't in the hospital, I spent almost every moment staring blankly at the TV. I didn't feel like talking to anybody and didn't even feel like getting up off of the sofa.

Ali was anything but silent or just lying around. He was twenty-one years old, and although he was an adult who was free and on his own out in the world, he acted like a ridiculously noisy kid. I remember lying on the sofa, staring at Daddy's little black-and-white television while Ali was being interviewed. He was loud, impossibly confident, and glowing as he trained for his fight against titleholder Sonny Liston for the biggest prize in sport, boxing's heavyweight championship of the world.

Liston was the most feared man in boxing. He'd knocked out everybody who'd faced him. Most boxing people thought there was no one who could seriously threaten his reign. The only person who was taking Ali seriously was Ali himself. When I saw Ali that first time, his voice roared and crackled from the huge, live world outside and punched a hole through the TV's rattling three-inch speaker. "Liston's too ugly to be champ," the voice said. "The champ should be pretty like me. I'm young, I'm handsome, I'm fast, I'm pretty and can't possibly be beat," the voice announced. The song the voice sang pulsed with menace, with grace, with an odd innocence, and with astoundingly playful intensity. When I heard it, I felt the glory train pass through me.

The next month, Ali surprised everybody by dominating, then easily knocking out Liston. And for the next several years, Ali handily whipped every person who stood in front of him in the ring. No one before had ever boxed the way Ali did. Even though I didn't know anything about boxing, I knew I was witnessing something and someone brand new in the world—someone who was different from anyone who'd come before.

Other fighters held their gloved fists up close to their ears and plodded back and forth like Rock 'Em Sock 'Em Robots. Ali carried his hands open, palms-up and down at his sides, and he danced quickly around the entire inside of the ring, which made him look beautifully in danger every moment he was boxing. The thing that kept him out of trouble was that he was the fastest (and most crazy-awake) man who'd ever fought.

In his fight with Brian London, at the beginning of round three, in just two seconds—one hippopotamus, two hippopotamus—Ali launched and landed a mind-numbing series of seventeen blows, punches thrown with such opponent-debilitating lightness, ease, and speed that they looked almost transparent; they took on a transparency. London bowed, he fell, he lay, sprawled on the canvas. The reason it took London a full two seconds to fall is that Ali's punches had come in such volume and with such velocity that they'd held London up. When Ali quit throwing, he stepped back and thrust his arms, godlike, above his head.

Sitting in front of Daddy's TV, I shook my head from side to side. How could anyone, much less a man as huge as Ali, a six-foot-three giant who weighed two hundred and ten pounds, how could he snap out more than eight concussively stiff punches in a single second? Not to mention that all the blows had struck a moving target. It didn't seem possible. But I had seen Ali do it. Or at least I had seen the tracers his gloves left in passing.

The one time it appeared that Ali would get beat wasn't in the boxing ring, but when he went up against the United States government. In 1967, Ali refused to be drafted into the army. He explained that he was a Nation of Islam minister and that his religion and beliefs didn't allow him to participate in the military.

Millions of people in America didn't like that, thought of him as a traitor and coward, and wanted him to go to jail. Millions of people in countries around the world admired the whomping-big courage it took to say no to the U.S. government, and Ali became their hero. Boxing authorities took away his world championship title and his license to box. The U.S. government took away his passport and wouldn't let him leave the country to make a living. In federal court, he was convicted of draft evasion and sentenced to five years in prison. But in June 1971, the United States Supreme Court unanimously declared that Ali was a conscientious objector who'd been wrongfully convicted.

Which cleared the way for him to do what he did this past week. In Zaire, Africa, on Tuesday night, October 30, 1974, two and a half months before his thirty-third birthday, "old man" Ali battled the young, undefeated, and seemingly invincible heavyweight king, George Foreman. Foreman's childhood hero had been Sonny Liston. Before the fight, almost everybody believed that Foreman, the hardest puncher ever in the history of boxing, might actually kill the "ancient" and "fragile" Ali.

That night, I went to bed with my transistor radio tucked up under my pillow. After I'd switched off the lights, I pulled it out, tugged the stiff leather strap up around my wrist, placed the leather-covered speaker against my ear, and slowly rotated the tiny plastic dial back and forth until I found a gravel-voiced announcer who was summarizing each round of the fight after it had been fought. A little before midnight, he said that, in round eight, after dominating almost every moment of the bout, Ali had knocked out the supposedly unbeatable Foreman.

The only person I knew who wasn't surprised was me. Ali immediately became the most popular man on the planet. Many people who had hated him came to admire him.

And now, because Ali has accomplished something as big and outlandish and worldly as all this, and because he's done so much that almost no one thought he could do, I've decided I can maybe do something pretty good, too.

Two

"YOU WANT TO DO WHAT?" Daddy says when I tell him my plans.

"All I need is a year, Dad. To find out."

"Dad?" he repeats. Like a lot of Southerners, I always call my father "Daddy." But I've been feeling pretty adult lately, and sort of worldly, too. So, at least in this moment, the word no longer fits.

"I need to find out what I can do, and where I fit. I'm almost eighteen. I can't afford to waste any more time."

My father softly laughs. It's Sunday afternoon and my sister, Carol, Daddy, and I are sitting around the dinner table after having stuffed ourselves on a big roasted turkey breast, steamed carrots, and boiled potatoes. Over the years since my mom died, Daddy's become a good cook.

"Davis," my father says, and I quit talking. Daddy almost always calls me "Dave." When he uses my regular name, that means he has something serious to say and he wants me to listen. Carol picks up dirty dishes and carries them to the sink.

"Son," my dad says, "I promised your mother I'd see to it you got a college education. I'd hate for you to work some no-account second- or third-shift job most your life. I've had to, and it's all because I didn't get that diploma that says I got the right to know somethin'. Life can get awful hard without a college degree."

As Daddy speaks, I remember stories my grandfather told me years ago—rich tales about Granddaddy's seven brothers and sisters, of orphanages he had to live in after his mother died, about brawling his way out of the Methodist Children's Home, about his years spent as a Merchant Marine. To me, tales of those times are as large as Aesop's Fables. Maybe even bigger, because they're about my own family. Stories of gold, of oranges and cinnamon, of storms, of shipwrecks, of ghosts.

I remember Granddaddy's other stories, too. Ones about his son's baseball days and how Daddy'd been a talented player who'd been offered a full-ride scholarship to Appalachian State Teachers College. And how Daddy chose to marry my mother instead.

Deeper than memory, I know what it was like for Daddy after they married. I know about two hundred newspapers Daddy delivered every morning before he went to work for ten hours in a factory that made corrugated boxes for cigarettes. I remember that whenever Daddy got home and hugged me, he was always wearing sand-colored khaki uniforms with black-and-white company patches my mother had sewn onto the breast pocket. And I remember Daddy going out a couple nights every week to try to sell newspaper subscriptions to new customers.

I know about better jobs Daddy was offered in Texas and Florida and other parts of North Carolina. He didn't take any of these because, as Granddaddy explained, "You kids woulda had to moved."

And maybe this is one hokey thing to say, but on a Sunday afternoon in early November 1974, for the first time in my life, I came to understand Daddy in some way other than as the four walls, the ceiling, and the floor around me: as the environment meant to protect me from the cold, tough, bone-splintering world outside.

Daddy doesn't have to say he supports my decision not to go to school next year. I understand that he does. My father will never be Muhammad Ali or John F. Kennedy or Babe Ruth or Neil Armstrong (or any of the other folks people idolize and buy books about). He will not escort the sun across the sky, won't walk only where he wants to go. But he'll allow me an opportunity he didn't have—the chance to try to do something with life besides work some "no-account job."

"I'll make it, Dad," I say. "You'll see."

And as I speak, I feel memories loosen like last autumn's leaves in a spring rain, sliding off the banks and into the muddy waters of the creek behind my father's house.

Three

I buy José Torres's Ali biography, *Sting Like a Bee*. In it,
I discover that my birthday and Ali's are the same, January 17. I start
working out the morning after our birthday—my eighteenth and Ali's
thirty-third. On Daddy's bathroom scales I weigh sixty-two pounds. I
get down on the floor and try to do my first-ever push-up. When I can't
squeeze out even one, I try to grind out some stooped on all fours, what
the gym teacher at Mount Tabor calls "girl's push-ups."

When I've worn myself out on about five of these, I run twice
around Daddy's backyard, my legs stiff from never having been used,
tripping a couple times in mole holes and almost falling. I finish my
day with a few overhead presses with the twenty-two-pound, baby-
blue plastic weight set Daddy'd tried to motivate me with when he
bought it for me after my mother died. The next couple mornings,
I'm so sore I can barely lift my arms over my head.

✦   ✦   ✦   ✦

ALL THROUGH the winter and spring, I stay with my workouts,
pushing myself so hard that I ache from neck to big toes all day,

every day. Soon I'm able to run five times around the yard—then ten, fifteen, twenty. After a couple months I sprint the last five laps and bound down the creek bank behind Daddy's house, splash through the water, and then drive up through the woods and briars and follow Silas Creek as it curves all the way down to Shaffner Park, creating my own ambling five-mile path.

By then I'm pumping out push-ups in big bunches: four sets of ten, twenty, then thirty-five, now fifty. Eventually, I get up to grinding out more than five hundred a day.

In January, I started with five sit-ups each workout. By April, I'm at five hundred sits, six days a week, every single week. Add a couple hundred crunches and leg raises on top of that.

Forcing myself to eat four giant meals every day, and adding a gallon of milk and a couple blenders chock-full of ground-up ice cream, bananas, and quick-weight-gain powder, I push the bathroom scales to 95, then 105, 112, 121. And I start growing in height. In May, when I go to Dr. Glenn's office for my yearly physical, I measure in at a humongous five foot five.

✦   ✦   ✦   ✦

WALKING PAST the bathroom mirror in just a pair of gym shorts, out of the corner of my eye I spot crisply defined torso muscles: *pectoralis, trapezius, latissimus dorsi, deltoids, rectus abdominis,* everything. For part of a second, I wonder who this person is in the mirror. Then I smile . . . though I'm still not sure this is my image.

✦   ✦   ✦   ✦

I START TAKING karate lessons because there's no boxing in town. I buy a uniform, go to class religiously, and work as hard as I can—I kick at the walls, punch the air and other students countless hundreds of times, and sweat and hurt for an hour and a half three nights every week.

My favorite sparring partner is Eddie "Racecar" Ford, a fast, gangly, utterly awkward guy only a couple inches taller than me. Racecar has pretty good kicks and okay hands. But what makes him fun to spar is that he's my equivalent of who Ken Norton is to Ali: a puzzle I can't easily solve. Racecar's so awkward it's almost impossible to predict the ways he'll move, or what shots he'll throw at you and when.

Soon I apply for a job at the convenience store up the hill from Daddy's house. The manager hires me to work second shift a couple nights a week, which allows me to support my Ali addiction—not only by giving me a few dollars, but also because, when I'm in the store by myself, I get to read all the boxing and martial-arts rags on the magazine rack. We sell a few paperbacks in the store, too, and I buy a copy of Norman Mailer's *The Fight*. It's the first real writing I've discovered about Ali and about the science of boxing; I had no idea something I was passionate about could be presented in such an accessible way—without destroying its power and mystery. Indeed, for me, Mailer enhances the beauty of pugilism by elegantly exploring it.

Between customers, in addition to reading, I do push-ups, stretches, a little shadow; think up, work on, and polish combinations until they gleam. It's the first job I've had. I'm surprised how much I enjoy it.

I recall getting in from work one night and spooning out a few vegetables Daddy'd left simmering for me on the stove, then carrying my plate into the den. While I stand with the plate in my right hand, forking stewed carrots and green beans into my mouth with the left, watching Johnny Carson while standing barefoot on the carpet, I throw three—count 'em, THREE!—whippingly wonderful and beatifically beautiful round kicks, all without touching my foot to the floor, cleanly snapping the heads from all three porcelain

Cupid statuettes who are sitting there minding their own business on a bookshelf high up over to the left of the TV.

I'm not upset by this (after all, consider the control it took to perform this feat); rather, I'm amazed—"Hey, wow, cool," I say— then, when I finish my final meal of the day and reach some level of post-martial sobriety, I try to repair my dead mom's old figurines with Elmer's wood glue.

When I'm not working out or pulling time at the convenience store, I'm studying Ali—on TV, in books or, most often, in free movies that roll behind my eyes. And I'm devouring all the convenience-store Ali magazines, as well as every book about martial arts and boxing that I can find. After studying *The Fight* time and again, an interest in real writing, in literary storytelling, starts to develop. I ask clerks in bookstores what fiction they enjoy most, and I find good nonfiction that way, too: by Harry Crews, Tom Wolfe, Gay Talese, Joan Didion, and later by Tim O'Brien, Norman Maclean, and Maxine Hong Kingston, all of whom open me further and further to the possibilities of the world of storytelling. And as I continue to grow, the world keeps getting bigger.

And then. I'm at 123, and '26, '28, '31, '35, and 140. What keeps me fascinated day in and day out is the belief that I'm doing something—shine on, shine on—and even more powerfully, I have the sense that in every moment there's something extraordinary to learn, some lush place to go that is throbbingly, achingly remarkable.

✦   ✦   ✦   ✦

TRAVELING FROM gym to gym and learning from everyone who'll spar with me, I like to outfinesse and outthink opponents, dropping my hands to my sides and dancing in circles just like Ali, but I don't like hurting anyone or getting hurt. In fact, the idea of hurting another person makes me sick to my stomach.

I buy a full-length mirror, place it against a wall in the basement, and shadowbox every day in front of it. Like Ali, with every punch I throw, I blow the air from my lungs with a short, hot, *fuuh* sound.

I dance and punch and kick and talk at the mirror, working to sound precisely like Ali. "No contest! no contest!" I shout. "Is that all you got?" I ask the mirror. "Rumble, young man, rumble," I proclaim as I get ready to start each round. "All night long!" I yell when up on my toes and dancing around the room. All these phrases are Ali's own personal favorites.

And maybe most inspiring to me is this line I've heard him say only once. "You say I can't do it because you can't," he proclaimed to some radio sports guy who sounded like his larynx had been replaced by an empty tin cup. "You say I can't do it because you can't," I say time and again. "But I'm not you."

With hands, feet, head, and mouth, no matter how difficult the skill or maneuver, I focus on making everything seem effortless and look beautiful.

Popping the air with blows too fast to count, I imagine lightning coursing through my limbs. I eventually get to where I can zing four, six, even eight crisp shots per second. And a funny thing happens because of all of this speedified "shoe shinin'," as Ali calls it. The heightened awareness that accompanies it expands my understanding of time; it teaches me how long that quick one second can be. All of which serves to open me further, and then further still, to the world, to its mysteries and possibilities.

Within months, I begin to feel I might be close to ready for the next step in my big-time, big-world plans.

Four

AFTER GRADUATION ceremonies, the Mount Tabor guys all leave for Myrtle Beach and a week of beer drinking and passing out under the sun. At the suggestion of my karate friend Bobby, who's Ali trainer Angelo Dundee's nephew, I load my car with workout gear and spend a long day driving five hundred miles from Winston-Salem to Ali's training camp in Deer Lake, Pennsylvania, where he's preparing for a world title defense against Joe Bugner, the British heavyweight titleholder.

"I'll see if I can get you in the ring with him," Bobby'd said, teasing me.

I didn't figure Bobby could make good on his promise, but suddenly here I am, in the fighters' cabin at Ali's training camp. And while I'm tugging on shining red Everlast trunks I've bought for this occasion, I listen to him through the dressing room walls, entertaining maybe fifty people who each paid one dollar to watch him train. "I'll prove to the whole world that I am not only the greatest boxer of all times," he says, "I am the greatest martial artist."

His voice is booming and musical. When he speaks, I feel it rumbling and rambling through my chest and belly. Listening to him makes me so nervous I shake a little and feel I need to pee. The old guy strapping a pair of rich-smelling red leather gloves on my arms looks at me and laughs. "He won't hurt a little white boy like you," he says.

I've finally learned not to think of myself as "little." The old guy is stooped, his face long, his eyes yellow with age. "Naw, he won't hurt you," he tells me again. "Not too bad, anyways."

He finishes tying the gloves, wraps athletic tape twice around the laces to keep them in place, then leaves the cabin. I pace back and forth, staring at the small room. The rough, scaly bark of the logs that comprise the walls makes me think of crocodiles lining up to eat me alive.

To escape the crocs I walk out the back door and step barefoot past boulders placed in a large circle around the cabin. On each rock a name has been painted by Ali's dad, Cassius Marcellus Clay Sr., in big red- and blue-trimmed white letters. I read the names— Willie "The Wisp" Pep and Sugar Ray Robinson, Jack Dempsey and Gene Tunney, Rocky Marciano and "Smoking Joe" Frazier, each man one of the best and most famous boxers ever. A rounded chunk of lichen-covered brown granite called Joe Louis has been granted the most honored position, in front of the main entrance to the gym. I listen to a train moaning a long way off. I watch the mailman come and go. "Good luck, son," he says, chuckling.

I walk back around the side of the cabin and climb the biggest boulder of all, a five-and-a-half-foot-high hunk of hard coal named after the very first black heavyweight champion, Jack Johnson. I stand on the rock, gloved hands at my sides. To calm myself and get my lungs started, I draw four deep slow breaths. With each inhalation, I swear I feel oxygen rush all the way down to my toes and out past my fingers. Closing my eyes, I imagine the very power of the cosmos flowing up from the boulder and into my body. *I'm ready*, I tell myself. *I'm entirely ready for this moment.*

Opening my eyes as I continue to breathe and to relax, I'm pretty sure what I've just said to myself is true.

Five

HE'S STANDING IN THE CENTER of his ring when I climb
the stairs and part the sky-blue, leather-encased ropes. Insect-
looking splotches of dried blood dot the rough, porous, beige canvas.
He's in process of wrapping his own hands, an act so uncommonly
self-reliant for a boxer that it's surely intimidated more than one sparring partner. I'm used to doing this myself, though, and so it doesn't
bother me. Plus I've carefully taped the balls of my feet so that I don't
need to worry about the canvas ripping or cutting them.

As I stare up at him, he comes into focus and everything else
blurs. His skin is unmarked and thoroughly without wrinkles, and he
glows in a way that cannot be seen in photographs or on television.
I realize once again that nobody else on the planet looks quite like
him. Right square in the face, he's nothing short of the world's most
beautiful and oversized kid.

"This man's a great karate master," he says to the crowd, pointing
a gloved left fist at me. His voice is young, innocent, in awe of itself.
I'm no master of karate or of anything else, but it makes me feel
good that he claims I am. Staring straight at me, he opens his mouth
steamshovel-wide. Then, in a voice directed not just to the people in

the room, but to the world at large, he shouts, "You must be a fool
to get in the ring with me. When I'm through, you gowna think you
been whupped by Bruce Lee." The crowd laughs and, though I feel
my face go red with embarrassment, I laugh with them.

"Are you scared?" he asks, looking at me hard and level. "Are you
scared?" he repeats. "Just think who you're with. How's it feel, knowin'
you're standin' here about to meet The Greatest of All Times?"

The bell rings and he dances to my right around the twenty-foot
square of taut canvas. Suddenly I'm no longer nervous. My legs are
strong and full of spring, and there's looseness in my movement. I
notice men, women, and kids in the crowd. Almost every single person is smiling with anticipation. He bounces from side to side in
front of me. I feel each step he takes tremble the ring, shoot into my
feet and up my legs. I bend to the right, toss a jab toward his belt line,
straighten, snap a long, tentative front kick up to his head. I figure it's
the first kick he's ever had thrown at him, but he pulls away as easily
as if he's been dodging feet his entire life.

He stops dancing and stands flat-footed in front of me, studying
my movements. Jesus, what a gigantic man.

I try to zing in a left jab. My arm is too short to reach him. His
eyes are snappingly bright, his face beaming and round and open.
Sliding toward him, I launch a second jab. He waits until my punch
is a half inch from his nose and pulls his head straight back. I punch
nothing but air and dreams.

He drops his gloves to his sides and cranes his neck way out in
my direction. Teasing by sticking out a long white-coated tongue, he
steps back to the ropes, taking a seat on the second strand where his
head is only a little higher than mine. With a brisk wave of gloves, he
motions for me to come in after him.

I block out spectators' laughs and skip inside his arms three half
steps; he's so close I feel his breath on my shoulder. I dig a round kick

into the soft area above his right hipbone and feel his flesh reshape to that of my shin. Now I see the opening I was hoping to create. I fake a jab and rocket from my crouch, blasting a spinning backfist-jab-left-hook combination straight into the center of his jaw. The punches feel so good I smile. People in the crowd *ooh* and *aah*.

He opens his eyes fried-egg-wide in pretend disbelief. He has never thought of me before, will never think of me as a fighter again, but for the next two seconds I deserve his serious attention. For two long seconds we are inseparably bound, whirling in a galaxy of electricity, each seeing nothing but the other man. For two week-long seconds I am flying. Then he springs off of the ropes and squashes me with one flyswatter jab.

I see the punch coming: a piece of gleaming red cinnamon candy exactly the size of a gloved fist. I try to slip to the side and can't—it's that fast. The back of my head bounces off of my shoulders. A chorus of white light goes off behind my eyes. A metal taste clouds my mouth, then comes a second, heavier thump as he catches me with a left hook I don't see. The spectators suddenly sound way, way off; my legs go to slow-turtle soup beneath me.

He knows I'm hurt and he steps back. His eyes go soft and round and kind, he slides an arm around my shoulders, we exchange hugs and smiles, and it's over.

But I've accomplished something I've never, yet always, believed I'd have the opportunity to do.

I have boxed with the world's greatest athlete, Muhammad Ali.

As we walk down the steps from the ring, my hero leans close to my ear and speaks in a way no man but my father has ever talked to me—softly, gently, almost purring. "You're not as dumb as you look," he says. It's a line he must've used half a million times. No matter how often I've heard him say it on TV, it makes me laugh every time.

"You're fast," he continues. "And you sure can hit to be *sssooo* little."

He may as well have said he was adopting me.

My legs shake hard, and I go dizzier than I think I've ever felt. But I stay in control long enough to say the one thing I hope will impress him most. With confidence I've learned from watching him on television and listening to him on the radio countless times over all these years, I say simply, "I know."

Act Two

All Things
Vibrate

Last Apple

One
MAY 1988

IN THE MONTH SINCE I MET ALI at his mother's and he gave me his phone numbers, I haven't called, not wanting to bother him, and feeling intrusive simply for having this access to his life. After all, it's not like I'm a close friend: hundreds of thousands, maybe millions, of people (this isn't an overstatement) have known Ali better than I. And as he himself admits, his kindness has been abused in hundreds of ways by untold legions.

On Wednesday, which is my day off from the store, when I'm through writing for the day, I tromp down to the basement and find two big boxes of newspapers and magazines I've carried with me as I've moved from place to place over the past two decades. I lug the boxes upstairs and sort through every yellowed, musty item: hundreds of articles that date from January 1964 to the present. Going through these stories and looking at old photos, I can't help but consider how the young Ali's seemingly endless energy had promised that he would never get old, and how in many ways he is now older than just about everyone his age.

Yet I don't feel bad for him. Ali's life remains huge. He seems less than fulfilled only when we see him in the smallest of ways, when we don't recognize that his Parkinson's and its aura of silence enlarge his legend and his life, that they complete his mythology. Most of the writing (and the talk) about Ali, not only now (about his health) but over the decades, has served to inaccurately limit him, to minimize him and his existence.

I don't have to be what you want me to be. One of the major themes of Ali's life is that he doesn't fall into our notions of who he is; he can't be capsulized, cannot be accurately defined. His life and spirit ooze out of the sides of the containers we try to stuff him in.

Sifting through these boxes of decay, I put aside a few items I care about—the program and ticket stubs from when Lyn and I tried to get married at the Shavers fight; a few posters and magazines; a copy of the classic 1970 Ken Regan head shot in which jeweled planets of sweat ride Ali's countenance like cold water poured on a hot copper frying-pan sky.

I carefully lay the bundle in my bottom desk drawer, reseal the boxes, and call Rahaman to ask if I can stop by for a few minutes.

✦   ✦   ✦   ✦

AT MRS. CLAY'S, Rock comes out to the car and helps carry the hundred-pound boxes up to the house. Sitting on the sofa, I show him a few items: newspaper and magazine pieces about the Liston fights; about Ali's conversion to Islam; the arrest for refusing military induction; the epic first battle with Frazier; the Supreme Court overturning the draft conviction; Foreman being voodooed by Ali; the Thrilla in Manila; the boxing lesson he gave Spinks in their second contest; a recent article about Ali buying buses for Chicago-area public schools (immediately after seeing a TV news story about how Cook County had no money for new buses, Ali sat down, wrote a check and mailed it, not using the gift as a tax deduction); and one about helping a young man dressed in a hooded dark sweatshirt and jeans who crawled out onto a high window ledge of a Wilshire Boulevard skyscraper in Los Angeles to kill himself. Police arrived, and as this man began yelling that Viet Cong guerrillas were coming to get him, a large crowd gathered in front of the building. Police officers asked him his name; he told them that it was Joe and that he was twenty-one years old; they tried to talk him in but quickly came to understand that they needed help from more appropriately trained professionals. They brought in an experienced psychologist. No help. A police chaplain talked to Joe at length. No luck. "Jump! Jump!" the crowd chanted as Ali slowly drove past, saw what was going on, got out of his car, and ran into the building. Ali leaned out of the ninth-floor window, promised to help Joe, and took his hand to bring him in. He bought Joe clothes, gave him money, got him counseling. "Joe knows my address," Ali later said. "I've told people to bring him to me. I'll help him. He knows he's got a home—my home."

Rahaman asks if an enlargement can be made of a *Newsweek* photo of Ali, himself, and their father with Gerald Ford at the White House. "Never seen a collection like this," Rock says. "Nothin' this big."

He gets up from the sofa and walks to a closet, coming back with a long cardboard tube. "These are my paintings," he says, popping a metal seal from the end of the tube. "Pictures of my brother."

He unrolls canvas after canvas, most crumbling with age and abuse, some water-damaged, a few in top condition. He has a strong sense of color and form, and I tell him so.

"Ain't nothin' compared to my daddy," he says.

I say I've heard that his father is a real painter.

"Aw, man, he paints be-yuuuu-tiful," Rahaman says, stretching the U sound like a giant rubber band. "Be-yuuuu-tiful," he repeats, leaning his head skyward as if speaking to an audience in the clouds. "I'll never be nothin' compared to Cash."

I tell Rock I need to head home. "Let me help with your boxes," he says.

"They're yours now," I say. "I wanted to give them to someone who'd take care of them. Too bad there's no museum to donate them to."

"Maybe there's gonna be," Rahaman says. "A fella's tryin' to start a boxin' museum in Louisville. Ali'll be in town this weekend to help out. We're all gonna meet at a gym downtown. Why don't you come?"

Two

SATURDAY AFTERNOON AROUND one-thirty, armed only
with a street number and a general idea of the building's where-
abouts, I drive past twice, first overlooking it, then saying, "Nah, that
can't be it," but maybe that tiny little box over there, over near the
river and nothing else except some abandoned warehouses with shat-
tered windows and a few wind-whipped scrub pines, that rundown
shack over there with the rutted dirt parking area and the fish market
behind it, maybe that's the gym. Yes, it is! The third time by, a black
Cadillac limo pulls into the parking lot and Ali's father, Cassius Marcellus Clay Sr., steps from the right rear door.

There's only one sign on the crumbling concrete-block building:
a swinging, creaking, rusted metal Royal Crown Cola advertisement
that at one time had been red, white, and blue. The windows have
been covered with sheets of plywood. Neon-green spray paint to the
left of the door reads, "BOO! SCARY SPOOK PLACE." If Ali saw this upon
entering, surely he had some fun with it. I imagine him putting on
an open-mouthed grimace. "Spook? I'll show ya a scary spook!" he'd
shout.

The first thing I notice upon opening the door is that the

bowling-alley-long, garishly lighted room smells ripe, slick, and
sweet with worn leather, old sweat, and oft-used liniments. In the
right corner stands a small, abused, blue-roped ring, its large-pored,
once-bleached canvas stained by body salts, blood, and Atomic Balm.
Near the rear of the room is a heavy bag, its thick, black leather cover
split open at the seams and nearly ripped from its body. Sinners have
certainly left this bag enlightened.

Today, though, this building is not a temple for the body, not
the abode of mad warrior monks in communion with the gods of
violence; the mood today is festive, up-front celebratory: red, yellow, blue, and orange balloons hang from the ring's corner posts;
rolls of red and white crepe paper have been strung throughout
the gym; three sliced watermelons and a punch bowl filled with a
thick pink fruit drink occupy a long card table near the center of
the floor. About seventy-five noisy people are present—men, women,
children—some dressed in Sunday best, others in T-shirts and jeans.
An eight-millimeter movie projector to the left of the ring is clacking
and spinning, throwing sepia-tinted images onto a blank area of the
crumbling plaster wall: films of the roughly sixteen-year-old Cassius
Clay jumping rope and blistering a heavy bag and a speed bag.

A couple of ancient boxing trainers are sitting on straw-backed
wood chairs beside the projector, one at each corner, as rooted,
gnarled, and self-contained as bonsai trees. Ali's boyhood gym mate,
opponent, friend, and former world heavyweight champion Jimmy
Ellis is standing to the right of the ring and beside one of the trainers, his big hand tender on the old man's shoulder. Ellis wears dark
glasses these days, having been blinded in the left eye in a final fight.

Ali's father has taken a spot next to Ellis. At five foot nine or
so, Cassius Clay looks like a miniature, much less benign, version
of Rahaman. In his youth, Cash had a darkly handsome rascality
about him; in his middle years, he was a brooding and troubled hard
mahogany knot of a man; in his seventies, he is bent, razor-thin,

and his eyes are deeply yellowed and clouded. Cash is crooning "For the Good Times" in a Vegas-fakewise voice that sounds of dusk and spent charcoal, performing for anyone who'll listen; at this moment, it's for a tall grinning white man who looks like a game show host or politician and who is being led around the room by a camcorder.

Ali is sitting on a folding metal chair beside Cash, appearing to ignore his father and looking as distracted as a ninth grader in algebra class on the day before spring break. Rahaman is to Ali's right, holding a clear plastic cup of punch and sporting a grin as big and goofy as the guy's with the camcorder—Rahaman's face intrinsically different in that it harbors none of that cracker's gleaming, old/new Southern "Can-you-believe-what-these-crazy-niggers-are-doin'?" half-submerged malice about it.

"This is borin'," Ali suddenly yells and stands, immediately commanding the attention of almost everyone in the room. He's dressed as some sort of emissary, in a manner beyond fashion, with quiet, near-timeless elegance: custom-tailored blue-pinstriped suit, lightly starched white shirt, royal-red patterned silk tie, polished black-leather uppers. For almost his entire public life, even Ali's haircut has transcended fashion: It's seldom been either short or long; today, it perfectly halos his features.

Ali steps up to the person nearest him, a burly, red-bearded, tough-acting country gent in a Hawaiian shirt. "Did you call me 'niggah'?" Ali yells.

The recipient of the accusation jumps back, startled and scared, instinctively putting his hands up and out to protect himself, then embarrassedly laughing. "Just joshin'," Ali says, looking sheepish and very young. He offers the man his hand, then whirls away, searching for the next soul to incite and cajole. Within seconds, he's playfully winging clownish punches at several people near him. Although he's in play mode, his moves come fairly loose and reasonably fast.

"Did you used to box?" he whispers respectfully to a middle-aged midget who's wearing big sunglasses and a black baseball cap with red stitching that reads ELVIS FOREVER.

He sneaks up behind several people, startling them with his cricket-in-your-ear trick, blows on the tops of heads, tickles the insides of palms as he shakes hands. He pretends to get knocked down by a blond eighty-pound girl who's wearing a pair of gold, queen-bed-pillow-sized boxing gloves that Ali has just finished autographing for her. As he rises from the floor, he turns and recognizes me and walks over and gives me his hand. "Didn't know you'd be here," he says, his tone determinedly innocent. "You surprise me." It's me who's surprised. With Ellis, his dad, Rahaman, the old trainers, and so many people in the room with whom he seems to share history, I'm stunned he knows who I am, much less that he pays any attention to me.

Just as he'd done in his yard the day we met, he motions to me with his eyes and puts his hands up beside his head. I dance to my left in exactly the style I learned from him twenty-five years before.

"You found a live one," somebody yells to Ali.

"I could be your daddy," Ali says to me, "if I was white."

Ali and I slip and move around the old wood floor for probably forty-five seconds. Like before, he seems a little surprised by my speed and style. As he tries to fire at me, I beat him to the punch. "You don't like black folks, do you?" he shouts. I find myself smiling. I feel good.

He points at a big blond late adolescent, a heavyweight, who's wearing a green polo shirt and who looks like a fraternity kid. The boy comes over and asks advice: "What's the best way to find a manager?" he says. "What do I do to go pro?"

Ali's answer is to pump a jab toward the kid's chin. The boy is put off for only a moment. Ali throws a second punch, then waves the kid in with both hands. The boy hesitates a moment, then launches slow, careful punches and slips mechanically but nicely as Ali throws back.

"Do the shuffle, Champ," I shout. For two seconds, he is once again hidden rhythm's dancer: his shiny street dogs blur into his own private dance step.

After thirty seconds of moving around with the college kid, Ali motions toward the ring and removes his jacket. I'm sure he must be joking, but he picks up a pair of licorice-colored Everlasts and walks to the ring apron.

As he steps between the ropes, he pulls his tie from his neck and the sixteen-ounce sheaths of leather are strapped onto his wrists. "Gowna do five rounds," he yells to people gathering ringside. The volume level in his voice has greatly increased. And the sound no longer issues from high in his throat; there's roundness to his words.

"Gowna teach you what it's all about," he says to his smiling opponent, then turns his back, unable to suppress a smile himself.

In his corner, the big grinning cracker with the camcorder pulls Ali's shirt tail from his trousers; the top button remains fastened. No one anywhere produces a mouthpiece; someone somewhere shouts "*ding*," and then it's actually happening—for conceivably the last time ever, sick old Muhammad Ali is really boxing.

A slow-moving cockroach of sweat crawls fat down the small of my back. Although in some ways I don't want to watch, and feel almost ashamed to be a witness, I have to admit to myself that I ache to know if he can still really do it.

Three

FOR THE FIRST THIRTY SECONDS, I want to wince with each blow thrown. Ali doesn't seem able to get up on his toes; his balance doesn't look good. He regularly slings quick-seeming jabs, but every punch misses. I believe the frat kid may be holding back in order to avoid hurting our ailing legend.

Suddenly, one minute into the round, The Champ drops his gloves to his sides, exposing his chin, and when his opponent tries to reach him with punches, he pulls his head back and away, just like the Ali we remember, causing the kid to miss by less than an inch. I hear myself say, "Ooh," and find I almost immediately relax some.

At the beginning of round two, Ali's face is animated, centered, serious. "No excuses," he says to himself, looking toward the canvas. "No excuses," he repeats.

The kid comes out hard, apparently wanting to make it a real fight. He thumps Ali with stiff punches to the chin and to the chest. Ali covers up. "Keep movin'," he says. "Keep punchin'."

The college kid steps in to throw another shot and Ali stabs him with a perfectly timed, teeth-rattling counter jab that's as sweet as a bite from the last tangy apple of autumn. The kid's head is turned ninety degrees by the force of the blow. It's a quick, very subtle shot, not thrown for audience reaction; almost no one in the room recognizes that the kid has been stunned. Fifteen seconds later, Ali shivers the kid's legs with a straight right lead. "Don't hurt him, Champ," Rahaman yells, but there's no need: Ali has backed off.

The kid gets on his bicycle; for a few moments he wears the expression of someone who has just been given a bright first taste of his own mortality. Ali boxes the rest of the round at a level slightly above the boy's abilities (although the boy himself may not recognize it). With twenty seconds left, he zings in a series of eight jabs and a razor of a right, all designed to make only surface contact, but to confirm that, at least in this moment, he remains Ali.

The old master does three more rounds with less capable students than the frat kid (chasing a hugely rotund guy who's wearing glasses around the ring, spanking him on the seat of his workout pants instead of punching his face or his jiggling body; cartoonishly winding up and lampoonishly telegraphing all of his punches while letting a 140-pound pointed-nose novice push him around all-four square), then steps awkwardly from the ring and immediately begins to walk his great-granddaddy walk.

I take a seat with him on the apron. "H-h-how did I look?" he asks. He has to repeat the question twice before I understand. Both of his arms are shaking, as is his head. "D-d-did I surprise you?" He chuckles and nods, satisfied to have kept the world in orbit.

He trudges over to the refreshment table, looking for something to drink. The punch is gone. He pulls a chunk of watermelon from the rind, juice dripping between his fingers, stuffs it in his mouth, turns the entire half-melon sideways, and lets juice slowly drip into a cup, which he expeditiously drains.

He tugs on his jacket and, in front of a big mirror that's used for shadowboxing, takes probably five minutes to convince his fingers to knot his tie, showing no impatience. We walk from the gym into a thin mist. The sidewalk is empty. A wet and shining blue Chevy pickup with a camper attached to the bed is at the curb. A short, thin, older black gentleman wearing a straw hat and holding an umbrella is leaning against the truck. Ali walks to the Chevy stiffly, silently, and with great dignity. He has trouble getting into his seat on the passenger's side. I close his door. He waves to me.

"Be cool," he says. And then he surprises me once again. "Remain wise," he says. With a trail of blue smoke shining in the air, the pickup pulls from the curb.

Ali Offers
Vocational Advice

One
AUGUST 1989

"MY MAN," ALI SAYS, drawing a deep, noisy breath to make his voice strong and audible. "Glad to hear from you."

It's the first time I've spoken with him on the phone. I think I'm adjusting to his voice. I tell him that I've lost my job, money's tight, and that I'm writing a story about him which I hope to sell to a magazine and that I think he'll like it. And then I tell him that Lyn and the kids and I might move back to North Carolina. But before we do, I say, I'd like to see him again.

"Be here a few days," he says and coughs his wet cough. "Come on up."

"What if I bring Rahaman with me? You want me to bring your brother?"

"Don't matter. Come on," he says.

✦   ✦   ✦   ✦

A WHITE seventies convertible Cadillac I haven't seen before is parked under the redwood deck behind Mrs. Clay's house. The badly scratched plastic rear window has several fist-sized holes in it.

"Partner. Little buddy," Rahaman says as he lets me in the front door, grinning and laughing and reaching to hug me. "Ready to go? Let me get my stuff."

A frayed tan canvas workout bag is at the bottom of the steps. Offering to help, I follow Rock downstairs. As I round the corner, I'm a little startled to find old Cassius Clay Sr. slouched in the center of the floor with a couple of bored-looking, dirty-faced, pre-adolescent white kids and their own father, who's no less scruffy. Cash's balance isn't good; as he turns to watch me enter the room, he rocks on his heels.

In the seven, maybe eight times I've visited, this is the first time Cash has been here. I consider asking after Mrs. Clay, who's nowhere to be seen, but then think better of it. Cash and Mrs. Clay haven't lived in the same house for years. I figure that when they broke up, Ali bought houses for both parents.

Watching five-foot-nine Cash and thinking about his wife, who's maybe five-three, I can't help but wonder how this very-average-seeming couple created these two huge sons. Rock asks if I've met his father, then introduces me.

"Have you heard my father sing? Have you heard Cash sing?" he says. "My father can really sing. He's got a big voice, like Billy Eckstine."

On cue, Cash falls into "Rainy Night in Georgia," making broad, waving gestures with his arms, tilting his head at a slightly elevated angle, and gazing wet-eyed and with stylized profundity into the near distance.

"Don't you think my father can sing?" Rahaman asks, softly clapping a large hand on my shoulder. "Cain't he sing *goooood*?"

For no apparent reason, Cash abruptly stops crooning and begins to preach in a raspy voice. "Told him to quit boxin'," he shouts, his yellowed eyes wide and wild and a little glazed. "Shoulda made movies. He was bigger than anybody. Prettier, too, and smarter. I met Elvis—all pimply-faced, ugly next to Ali. Not smart, either."

As Ali's gentleness and pecan beauty were inherited from his mother, ash-black Cash endowed his eldest son with a crazed brilliance, a perennially anxious ambition, and an almost boundless need to be on stage (as well as the capacity and desire to pound people in the face). Now, Cash discontinues his sermon and spins into "For the Good Times."

Though Rahaman is standing beside me and I'm looking straight ahead and can't see him, I feel him grinning at his daddy, Cassius Marcellus Clay, that proud, high-styling, regally named painter and singer who, despite ambition and talent, surely stood zero chance of making it among the gentrified Louisville crackerdom of the 1930s and '40s.

"He's so *goooood*. Ain't my daddy *goooood*?" the younger brother of the world's most famous man asks again.

Two

ACCORDING TO ROCK and to the gas station map, it's a full day's drive from Louisville to the Ali farm in Berrien Springs, near the foot of Lake Michigan and maybe two hours around the base of the lake from Chicago. We stop to eat fast-food chicken and for Rock to buy grape sodas (I packed a thermos of iced tea from which I drink cup after cup), but otherwise drive straight through, listening to Aretha and Marvin Gaye CDs.

Rock sleeps and snores as I try to take in everything on both sides of the road. As we slow for the village of Ganges, Michigan, he wakes as we stop at the town's one stoplight. "All praises to Allah!" he suddenly shouts, his transmission inexplicably in a speedy gear. "Allah blesses me every day, blesses me all the time. Just think about all the good things he put in the world. Think how good that piece of chicken tastes when you put it in your mouth, think about that blackberry cobbler.

"Allah's been so good to me," he proclaims with his eyes closed, shaking his head from side to side. "Think about all that sweet, sweet pussy he's blessed us with. Oh, all the pussy I've had. Women all around the world. In Manila for Frazier, this sweet young Filipino girl. A Muslim, too. Almost brought her home. Oh, so sweet. All praises to Allah."

Soon, a few silver hills rise in the distance on both sides of the road, and then we drive beside a shallow rocky river where I crank down my window, slow the car, listen to the sound of tumbling water. On the right, a green metal sign reads: VILLAGE OF BER-RIEN SPRINGS, HOME OF CAREY NATASHA BELL, MISS BLOSSOMTIME 1988. To our left stands a dam with a big wood waterwheel. We cross a bridge over the river, climb a steep short hill, and enter the township.

Berrien Springs is so small that after you've driven through it once you might not know everything in town, but you definitely won't get lost. Rahaman tells me to make a left at the stoplight at the top of the hill. After a short distance he says, "Go left again, across from the Starlite." For some reason, he thinks that's funny. He grins as if apologizing and laughs and laughs.

We turn where a sign that says STARLITE fronts a weeded and otherwise empty field, then go maybe five miles down an unlined tar and gravel road through a neighborhood of one-story 1950s and '60s ranch-style brick houses, at the end of which are two stone pillars, an open black wrought-iron gate and a big white sign with large gilded yellow letters. MUHAMMAD ALI FARMS, the sign reads.

We move slowly through the gate and down a long asphalt drive-way lined with older rhododendron, birch, and maple. The driveway winds to the left. We pass several white wood buildings and a barn and look down on a little lake and, beyond that, a thin river that flows slowly, muddily past gently sloping white-fenced fields (in the Ken-tucky tradition): a picture postcard of an American farm. We pull behind the modest two-story white frame house and park between a new, shining blue Cadillac sedan and a brown-and-beige convertible Rolls-Royce. Ali's Winnebago and a brown Chevy Blazer are to our left in front of a big children's playground with a slide that's probably thirty feet high, a carousel, and park-size swings that have recently been painted shining candy-apple red.

A tall, strong, light-skinned woman maybe a few years younger than me and dressed in a flowing beige cotton tunic greets us at the back screen door. "Hi, I'm Lonnie Ali," she says, offering a tentative business-style handshake before she hugs Rahaman. It's easy to understand Lonnie's reticence when shaking hands: Ali has been taken so many times by so very many hustlers. Oh, what she must have witnessed married to the world's most famous (and accessible) soft touch.

Like Ali's mom, his wife's oval face is splashed with a galaxy of freckles, and as is true of Mrs. Clay, Lonnie's loosely pinned hair has an aura of redness about it. It's easy to understand Ali's attraction to Lonnie; he has always been closer to his mother than to anyone else. Lonnie has an astute, yet girlish and musical voice, exophthalmic eyes, and, like her husband, a dead-flat-on and very strong, deep way of looking at you.

We enter the house through a back porch, then a small kitchen with yellow linoleum floors and countertops, a little white wood table, and knotted oak cabinets exactly like those in the kitchen in my dad's house. "Muhammad's asleep," Lonnie says.

She's the first Ali intimate I've heard call him by his first name. She leads us into a large den with white walls, wheat-colored carpet, a stereo, two overstuffed beige couches, a silent TV that takes up nearly one whole wall, a mahogany desk almost entirely covered with stack upon stack of blue and yellow and green and pink pamphlets, and, against the right side of the steps that lead upstairs, a big ornate Lebanon cedar trunk on which a small brass plaque under the lock reads, MUHAMMAD ALI MAGIC.

Lonnie says, "This heat bothers Muhammad. Tires him out."

It tires me, too. Even in here out of the sun, it's maybe ninety degrees. A small rotating silver-colored fan whirs on the kitchen table and a large green model clunks and rattles in the window behind the desk. It's surprising that a guy who has made over one hundred million dollars lives in a house that hasn't been air-conditioned. And although the den furnishings are—— comfortable, no one would call them posh.

Rock and I take seats on a sofa and Lonnie steps out to the kitchen, returning with sweating glasses of lemonade. We sip our drinks and talk about a Gary Smith–penned *Sports Illustrated* cover story I'd shown Ali the April day it had first appeared on newsstands. Lonnie, Rock, and I now agree it was anything but fair to him, or accurate. I ask Lonnie how she reacts when people treat Ali as a falling-down cripple.

"People believe what they read in the press," she says. Then: "I just wish some writer could tell the truth about Muhammad, could find a way to get to his soul."

As she says this, I silently resolve to craft the best Ali stories that anyone will ever write: *I will become The Greatest Ali Writer of All Times—I outflash Tom Wolfe with a pyrotechnic display of lexical skill. Arms pointed skyward in victory, my feet explode into the shuffle over the kayoed Norman Mailer. Twenty thousand fans in the Garden erupt into singular applause as I hop through the ropes, leaving the ring with the protection of New York's finest.*

We finish our lemonades and chat for a while, then Lonnie says she has laundry to do and, as she escorts us back through the kitchen, suggests Rock and I take a tour of the farm while Muhammad sleeps. "Floyd's out there somewhere," she tells Rock, motioning toward a window in the direction of the barn. "Maybe he can show Davy around."

I can't help but chuckle. She looks at me, wondering why I've laughed. "I'm sorry," I say. "It's just that it amazes me how kind you all are, how much you accept strangers into your lives."

The truth is, I'm not surprised by that at all. How could I be?

This is the family of Muhammad Ali, who feels he belongs (*wants to belong*) to every man, woman, and child in the world. The real reason I laughed is this: *Davy!* she said. *Davy!* Lonnie called me. Not Davis. Not David, either, or even Dave or Dennis, all of which I'm used to being mistakenly tagged. Nobody's ever called me "Davy." At least no one since my great-grandmother Mandy, who, when I was little, regularly laughed her bold crackling laugh and called me "Davy Crockett." But Mandy's been gone for almost a decade and a half. And I'm thirty-seven years old. *Davy!* A grown man being called Davy. I think I like it.

Rock opens the back door and heat slaps us flat on our faces. As we walk across the asphalt parking area, I ask if it's true that this was originally Al Capone's farm. Rock shakes his head as if I'm the only Ali fan he's ever listened to. "Man, it's hard to believe you sometimes," he says, which I take to mean the Capone rumor is true.

We move into the scant relief of dappled shade from expansive oaks around the barn. With a creak, Rock pushes open the long, rusted barn door and we step through a weak shaft of light in which dust motes swirl and shine. It's so bright in the sun that it's hard to see in the barn, a little like putting your head under clouded water. After a few seconds, I make out shapes; within a half minute, apparitions take form. Hanging on rough exposed beams and walls and littering the ground are framed 1960s and '70s paintings and photographs of Ali and a few large tarnished trophies.

"Looks better, don't it?" comes a voice from behind.

"Floyd Bass, my man," Rock says before he whips around, grinning his grin.

I turn and see a figure in dirty gray pinstripe coveralls standing in direct light just outside the doorway. "If you don't know Ali," Floyd Bass says as he pulls off a brown work glove, then snaps a greasy pink rag from his pocket, "it's hard to understand why he don't care about this stuff."

Bass moves out of the sun and across the packed dirt floor and, with the rag, knocks a fat brown spider and its web from a grungy, dented loving cup that bears the inscription, ATHLETE OF THE CENTURY—MUHAMMAD ALI.

Floyd Bass doesn't look much like a Floyd, I think. A guy with his countenance should have a name like Isaiah or Abraham or Hezekiah. The name Floyd seems mundane for such an intriguing-looking man.

Floyd Bass has smooth, glowing, unwrinkled skin; shining eyes the hue of sand and October sea; a curly halo of slightly receding hair that has gone prematurely white (as if it has been illuminated); a short round beard the color of both shadow and light; a perpetual-seeming crinkled smile; a whisper-soft, even-timbered voice; and a general demeanor that suggests he has visited the mountain and come down changed. How could anyone look and sound more like the perfect handyman for Ali the whispering mystic?

"Until I started working with this," Bass says of the memorabilia around us, "it was all stacked over in that corner, all covered with pigeon shit." He points to empty nests in the rafters. "Even now, when most of his stuff's long gone, when some fan shows up with a wife and kids, Ali'll give 'em a trophy or some old gloves or a painting or somethin'. He does it all the time, even now. It's amazing he's got anything left."

Rahaman introduces me and asks Floyd Bass if he has time to show us the farm. Bass takes off his other work glove and stuffs the pair in his right pocket. "I'll give you the ten-dollar tour," he says, smiling as if this is an inside joke.

He leads us through a side door and past a pen of shaved sheep panting in the heat, then through a scorched yet sweet hay-smelling pasture and down to the narrow river, where Bass shows us that it curves around three sides of the Ali property and tells us that the farm is eighty-eight acres of the best bottomland anywhere.

Heading back toward the main house, we climb a gently hilled pasture through hip-high grass. Cresting the hill, we step onto the driveway and pick beggar's-lice and shake other seeds from our clothes. Anxious to see if Ali is awake, I start for the house. "Whoa, not so fast. We've got one more stop," Bass says, winking as he turns toward four white shacks near the curve in the driveway.

Except for being smaller, the buildings remind me of ones you see in old "B" westerns, movies set in frontier ghost towns with names like Tombstone. We head for the next-to-the-last shack, which has a vacant horse stall attached to the right side and double swinging doors not unlike those to a saloon in one of those western movies. There's a window near the center of both splintered and crumbling doors; the glass on each has been painted black. The only other window I see is around the left side of the building; it's smeared with long-dried orangeish mud and covered from the inside with sheets of newsprint that make it impossible to peer within. Bass pulls a heavy jangle of keys from a silver chain hooked to a loop attached to his left pocket and finds a big old rusted iron key, which he inserts in the blackened lock. He leans his right shoulder and foot into the left side of the door, shoves it open, and suffers a shower of rotted wood before he steps to the side, waving Rock and me through.

Badly chipped and rotting floorboards, water-damaged sheetrock walls, a strong smell of mildew, no visible electric lighting. And no tommy guns left by a former owner. There is, however, a heavy bag, its big black leather bulk hanging sure and straight and silent in the center of the room. No! Not just a bag—this is *The Bag*, the Famous Muhammad Ali Heavy Bag, the one he'd had custom-made for the Foreman bout (bags packed in the usual way damaged the older Ali's delicate, punch-weary hands) and continued to use through The Thrilla in Manila and for the remainder of his fistic career.

Near the rear of the stubby room, opposite the big bag, is a thick black wood platform from which hangs a brand-spanking-new shining fire-engine-red Everlast 4204 Astro, one of the fastest speed bags in existence, its bladder freshly pumped with air and ready to sing. Across the floor from the bags is what's left of a twenty-foot ring, the canvas filthy with ancient sweat and farm dirt, the formerly flexible blue leather covers on the rough braided ropes now brittle, ripped, and fading, the ropes themselves sagging into one another like kudzu vines after the first winter frost. Could this be the same ring in which, several lives ago, I sparred with Ali when he ached with beauty, and from which I was led looking freshly electrocuted?

"Mosta this stuff came from Deer Lake when the camp people took over," Bass explains, still brushing wood particles from his coveralls.

"What camp people?" I ask.

"The old boxing gear got moved out and the training camp's been turned into a center for abused kids," he says. "I'm not sure anybody anywhere likes children as much as Ali."

I nod. "His radar sure is tuned to kids," I say. "Does Ali really use this stuff?"

"Sometimes," says Bass.

Wanting to feel an even greater connection with Ali, I step to The Champ's renowned heavy bag and spring punches into its musty old hide as Bass and Rock watch. With each shot thrown, I imagine that prisms of light follow my fists. "Not bad," Bass says, "for a white boy."

Rock thinks this Ali-inspired line is funny as can be. He laughs and laughs and makes a hissing sound between his teeth.

We lock the gym and Bass asks if I'll drive down the road to St. Joseph to grab a soda or something. "Don't worry about missing him," he says of Ali. "He won't wake up no time soon."

Although Bass's comment makes me a little uncomfortable and I remain uneasy about leaving, we clamber into my car and go up the long driveway and out onto a scarred and pitted country highway, past the campus of Andrews University (an evangelical Christian college to which, Bass says, Ali walks to talk with/debate/counter-evangelize seminary students), then grove after grove of dwarf apple and peach trees, grape orchards, and the fresh-shit smell of fertilized fields. We pass the St. Joseph River yet again, round a curve, and suddenly we're smack in the middle of a long, low, garish retail strip.

Bass suggests we stop at the St. Joseph McDonald's. Inside, we order fries and sodas, a fish sandwich for Rahaman, chicken for Bass. We take flimsy purple seats at a purple-and-yellow plastic table and I ask Bass how he met Ali. "I was livin' in the Silicon Valley," he says. "Made me a fortune in microchips—and then lost it. Got real depressed. Decided to come home, thought that might improve my luck."

As he's speaking, Bass's face becomes incongruous with what he's saying: his smile goes crinkled, fuzzy, and enigmatic; his skin takes on a sheen and becomes more richly colored; and although he doesn't move in his seat, his features edge themselves toward his listeners. "Moved in with my mother," he tells us. "Can you imagine that? A man my age. Didn't want a job, couldn't find one anyway, just about decided I'd go over to the oven, turn on the gas, and stick my head in. That's when I read in the paper that Ali was movin' to Berrien Springs full time. For years, everybody knew he had the place—he'd come sometimes to rest up. A few days after that story, I ran into him here, right here under the Golden Arches."

Bass must see my surprise that he met The Greatest of All Time while eating at a McDonald's. "Ali knows there's always people here," he explains, "always somebody to talk to. He walks over and gets a hot chocolate or a coffee, maybe an ice cream."

"*Walks?*" I say. "You mean from the farm?" It's easily over ten miles from the Ali place to here. And that's taking the main road. Getting off the highway, I'm sure the distance would be greater.

"Yep," says Bass. "Coupla, maybe three times a week when he's home." At great-granddaddy Ali's pace, these McDonald's trips must take most of the daylight hours—especially since he is, after all, who he is: his progress surely gets blunted every couple hundred yards (mostly to his delight, I'd bet) by people who stop their vehicles to say hello or ask for autographs.

"In this heat," I say, "even in July and August, does he do it? Does he still walk all this distance?"

Bass nods. "None of us want him to, least of all Lonnie. If the sun don't get him, we all worry he'll get run over. But Ali's just gonna do what Ali's gonna do. I tried to tag along a few times, thought he might want the company. After a mile or two, he sent me home. Said he wanted to be alone.

"Anyway," Bass goes on, "I met him here and we talked and I told him I used to box. Told him I became a civil rights activist because of him. Asked if he thought he might need some help around the place. I came over that Saturday and raked a few leaves and burned the piles. Then I started doing a few odds and ends for him, not takin' money for my work. Next thing I know, I'm workin' thirty hours a week."

Bass laughs, scoots his chair back, gets up. Standing over me, his face goes even brighter than it had already been. "I swear to you," he says, "that man saved my life." He turns from the table and, as he does so, I note that he's bald in precisely the spot Franciscan brothers shave their crowns to provide an unobstructed pathway through which to receive heavenly illumination.

He quickly returns with plastic salt and pepper shakers in his right fist. "Every day," he says, "that man makes me glad to be alive, glad I know him."

This sounds like something Floyd Bass has wanted to say for a while. "Hell, I'm glad to be part of the same species as him," Bass says. "I tell you, that man's a real live angel."

"Yeah, yeah," Rahaman says with tartar sauce in his mustache. Chomping on a bite of fishwich, he's nodding. "He's my own brother."

He swallows hard. "I mean, I know he got the same daddy as me, and the same mama—and he come from between her legs. My whole life, I been watchin' him—watched him get exactly where he is right now. But that's the way I feel about him, too."

What a life Ali has had. I recall a television documentary in honor of Aaron Copland on his eighty-fifth birthday. "There is no greater reward than having been able to make my living creating something that will outlive me, something that's lasting," the old composer told an interviewer. Our species has perhaps an innate desire for continuance. Most of us grope for immortality in religion, through our children, in possessions we collect, in names we give fellowships and buildings, through our work, on tombstones. Artists grabble for immortality through art and/or fame. The first place Muhammad Ali groped for his was through the renown he garnered in the ring. In the history of the world, Ali became more famous than anyone else had been in his/her own lifetime. Way back in 1975, Wilfrid Sheed wrote with more than a little awe that Ali's likeness hung in African mud huts. And surely, this was (and is) true. Just as certainly, it hung on walls in Kiev, Detroit, London, Mobile, Kuala Lumpur, and L.A., as well as in Tokyo, Cleveland, Tangier, Beijing, Tel Aviv, Bogotá, Sydney, Mexico City, and Kathmandu. Ali became known and honored in virtually every nation, city, town, and village on the planet.

In 1982, when I was a student at Wake Forest University, the poet Robert Pinsky made a visit to campus and told a story of a trip to the Sahara. He and his wife hadn't seen anyone for miles and miles, days and days, dune after dune. They passed a herd of goats and a boy of about ten years. In Arabic, the boy asked the poet where he lived. When the poet answered, the boy enthusiastically repeated, "America," and danced in a circle around his small herd. "Muhammad Ali! Muhammad Ali!" he shouted. The poetry of the name. Muhammad Ali. To me, it doesn't much matter that the words are Islamic. The music of the name itself, the sheer beauty of the sound, is what I find most interesting. Indeed, I believe that as long as there are human beings it's likely the name will be spoken.

Inevitability. "The whole point of composing," Copland told fellow composer David Del Tredici, "is to feel inevitable." It now often feels as if Muhammad Ali had to come along when he did.

What would Ali himself say about this? Ever since I began watching him, he has always carried himself as if centered in his own destiny, as if he is doing that which he is intended to do. Ali has been a creature of earth and of sky: he has acted as though he owns everything, and nothing. He has claimed to be The Most Important Person to Have Lived, and the simplest of men. He has seemed the world's oddest wise man, and some kind of strange, impossibly naive, utterly retarded, perpetually and entirely narcissistic virgin. Indeed, it's not overstatement to suggest that he has always been a world unto himself. Yet, in surprisingly new ways, never more so than now.

These things considered, Ali's sojourns to the Golden Arches, to that global emissary of sales hyperbole ("Billions and Billions Served Worldwide"), make perfect sense. Could anyone invent a more insanely appropriate location for Ali's monk/handyman, Floyd Bass, to propose the divinity of Planet Earth's First Truly International Human?

Three

AS WE LEAVE MCDONALD'S, Bass asks to swing by the house of the county sheriff, a short and round, red-cheeked man of maybe fifty-five, who leans across his front-porch banister and promises that he'll have deputies look out for Ali. "We'll convince him there're better places to take his exercise than a patch of skinny country highway," he tells Bass.

I understand and admire Bass and the sheriff's concern for Ali. Like so many people, however, they're treating Ali as if he isn't capable of making his own decisions. The effect of their kindly yet covert act, as has often been true throughout Ali's life, is to deprive him of the opportunity simply to *be*. Not an hour before, Bass theorized Ali's celestiality; now he has suggested that the man—oops! angel—can't make it across the road on his own. This isn't any reason for me to get angry: these guys hope to keep Ali from being squashed by a careening eighteen-wheeler, from becoming The Most Famous Roadkill of All Times. Yet their reaction seems unfortunate.

Until I stop to consider the situation from another perspective: Bass and the sheriff, although they may not be able to say it, or feel no need to do so, simply wish to protect that which they regard as, well, if not sacrosanct, at least singular and extraordinary. They want to do what they believe is best for someone they care about. And for sure, I don't have any quarrel with that. There are so many ways to think about almost everything. And none of them is nearly as round as the reality.

When we return to the house, Bass gets into his rusty old International pickup and heads for home. I pull two choice items from my car's backseat for Ali to autograph and promise myself that I won't take advantage of his munificence by asking him to sign anything again for a long, long time. As Rock and I go in the back, on the door there's a note from Lonnie that says she's at the grocery store. Inside, Rock picks up a remote control from the coffee table; the TV blinks on to CNN. I'm not interested in watching: my antennae are on Ali alert.

Within minutes, a pair of big flat bran-color feet slowly descend the staircase, followed by the torso and head of the world's best-known man, who's wearing wrinkled black slacks and a freshly pressed and starched black safari shirt that has a yellow laundry tag stapled to a low buttonhole. His face is swollen and his hair needs combing. He sucks a deep breath. "My man," he says, seeming to summon language from an almost forgotten recess.

He gives me his hand and, as we shake, tickles the inside of my palm with his middle finger. I laugh and say, "Man, you never quit, do you?"

Without acknowledging Rahaman or saying anything further to me, Ali wades away to the kitchen, returning with a sloshing white mug of very black coffee, which he carefully places on the table before he falls back on the sofa between his brother and me. He doesn't look at either of us, but leans forward, reaching for a sugar bowl on the table. He tries to clear his throat, turns his eyes toward me, and points questioningly at his cup.

"No thanks, Champ," I tell him. "Rock and I drank about a gallon of iced tea maybe an hour ago."

Ali nods, snorts, coughs his wet cough, takes a spoon from the sugar bowl, and dumps spoonful after spoonful into his cup and onto the table, nine to ten to maybe even eleven mountainous servings altogether. After a fat noisy slurp, he sets his dripping mug back on the table.

"Glad you're here, glad to see you," he says and gives my leg the gentlest squeeze in the hollow above the knee. He gets up again and walks over to his desk, motioning me to follow.

"Sign a thousanda these a day. Take some, give 'em to your friends." He picks up a stack of little green pamphlets and hands them to me. I look down at the pieces of paper in my hand. IS JESUS REALLY GOD? reads the thick bold script in the center of the page. Above Jesus's name is Ali's signature and the month and year, with a space left in the middle for the date. "If anybody else tried to give these to people, they wouldn't take 'em or they'd throw 'em away," he says. "I sign 'em and they take 'em home and keep 'em."

He grabs a big gold permanent marker, from which he removes the cap, then takes his seat behind the desk, waiting for me. I'm a little startled by this reaction—that he knows I want him to autograph some things—but I unfold a two-by-three-foot poster that used to hang on my bedroom wall in my dad's house and spread it across Ali's desk. It's a blown-up copy of the famous photograph in which Ali contorts George Foreman's features with a staff-straight right (a halo of sweat lifts from Foreman's face with the impact of the blow; Ali glows like Shiva in the paintings in the *Bhagavad-gita*). Ali stares at the photo an interminable moment; it's not hard to tell that he doesn't want to sign. Some part of him is no longer proud of the ways he has hurt other human beings.

"Davis Miller is my name," I say. "D-A-V-I-S." As he continues to hesitate, I open my mouth to tell him that I understand; he doesn't have to sign. But now, his hand is on the paper. "To Davis Miller," he writes, "LOVE, Muhammad Ali, 8-3-89."

He carefully refolds the poster and hands it to me, then autographs the fight program I've been keeping since Lyn and I tried to get married at the Shavers bout. He snaps the top on his marker and pushes it to the only corner of the desk not inhabited by Muslim tracts.

"You believe in ghosts?" he asks for no reason that I can determine.

"No," I say.

"I'll show you a ghost. I'll make you believe." From his magic trunk he pulls a thin white cloth, which he places over the spilled coffee and sugar. He waves his hands across the table and says, "Arise, ghost, arise," in a foggy-sounding voice. The cloth quavers and a coffee-stained peak shakingly appears in the middle.

"Told you there's a ghost in the room," he says.

I ask: "Do *you* believe in ghosts?"

"Do you?" Ali says.

"Yes," I say. I study his face. He doesn't seem surprised. "You're a ghost," I say, "or I guess I mean the images people have of you—what they, and me, and even you, say you represent—those are ghosts. And I'm a ghost, too. The way I want—no, *feel a need* to get something about you on paper, to write the best story in me, and have it carry on after my body is gone. That's being a ghost. But it's not the only way I'm one. We're all ghosts. Walking, talking spirits. All of us. In countless ways. All the time."

"*Maannn*, that's powerful," he says. "Heavy. You oughta write a book."

Ali, Rahaman and Floyd Bass playboxing in
Berrien Springs, Michigan (August 1989)

The Zen of Muhammad Ali: Part One

One

DECEMBER 1989

THE FIVE-THOUSAND-ROOM Mirage Hotel and Casino is celebrating its grand opening. Directly across from the main entrance, a fifty-six-foot-high manmade waterfall suddenly rumbles and hisses and spits piña-colada-scented, flaming natural gas thirty feet up into the air. On Las Vegas Boulevard, dozens of cars stop to watch the "volcano" while a gaping, yelling crowd of hundreds leans against guardrails on the sidewalks. A group of twenty Tibetan Buddhists, in red and yellow robes and leather sandals, stands in seeming serenity near the street. Their shaved pates gleam in the reflected light of the flames.

Just inside the hotel, a pair of near-life-sized brass mermaids sprawl in lascivious poses atop marble platforms, boldly thrusting shining bare breasts into the faces of passersby. A bone-thin scraggly-white-haired woman in her seventies sits on one of the platforms, watching her feet. Two Middle Eastern men in their late forties take turns at the other statue, snapping photos of each other pretending to suckle slightly post-adolescent nipples.

Behind the registration desk, there's a blue-watered aquarium rich with six- and seven-foot twisting sharks, and to the left of the main casino, a white glass-enclosed room in which Siegfried and Roy's white Bengal tigers prowl and shit and sleep. At feeding times, the animals are removed from public display.

These meretriciously American visual stimuli were chosen and implemented by Steve Wynn, the owner of the Mirage. B-movie-handsome Wynn has rainforest-thick black hair, sun-bronzed skin, snapping reptilian black eyes, and *retinitis pigmentosa* that will cause his field of vision to narrow and narrow until he eventually goes blind.

I've recently been made boxing editor at *Sport* magazine and I'm at the Mirage as the magazine's representative for the third Sugar Ray Leonard–Roberto Duran fight. What I care about more than Leonard, Duran, my ringside seat, the Mirage, Steve Wynn, or Las Vegas is that Ali will make an appearance at the fight.

I've often hung out with Ali since that Easter Friday when I first met him at his mom's house. And I've written big-magazine stories about our developing friendship, several of which have served to launch my career. Because of my childhood idol, after over a decade and a half of trying, I've found my voice (and my great subject). I've become a writer.

On my first visit down to the Mirage casino, right off I spot a familiar face. "Lonnie," I call as she walks past, heading for the penthouse elevator. "Lonnie Ali," I say as she turns around. "I hope you remember me. I'm Davis Miller."

"Oh, Davy. Sure I remember you. I was just going up to the room. Come on with me. Muhammad'll be happy to see you."

✦   ✦   ✦   ✦

"MUHAMMAD, you have a visitor," Lonnie says as she opens the door to the top-floor suite. "It's Davy."

Yeah, I like it. I really do like being called Davy. Going through life with a first name that's also a last name makes you feel that you have something to live up to. A nickname like Davy allows me to dress down some.

Ali is sitting on a small white sofa near full-length windows that overlook the east side of town. He's wearing a pair of well-pressed navy pinstripe slacks and a white V-necked T-shirt that has a couple of nickel-size holes in it, one of which reveals whorls of thin white hair on the left side of his chest. He's munching a big blueberry muffin that looks small in his fist. He's the heaviest I've seen him. His waist is thick; I'd guess he's at about 265. "My man," he says. "How's Loovul?"

I remind him that I don't live in Kentucky anymore. He seems not to take interest; his eyes go dull. He gets up from his seat and walks stiffly to the windows. The label of his white cotton briefs is sticking out of the top of his trousers. He motions me to follow.

"Look at this place," he says, whispering. "This big hotel, this town. It's dust, all dust. Steve Wynn, thinkin' he's some kind of pharaoh, buildin' this big tombstone like it'll make him immortal."

His voice is so volumeless that the words seem to be spoken not by Ali, but by a specter standing in his shadow. "Elvis, Kennedy, Martin Luther King, they all dead now. It's all only dust."

We stare down at the sun-bleached town. In the middle distance, just before the edge of the Spring Mountains, a military fighter, dwarfed by the craggy rock mountain faces, touches down at Nellis Air Force base. "Go up in an airplane," Ali is saying, seemingly unrelated to the fighter jet, his voice rattling with phlegm and ether. "Fly real low, we look like toys. Go high enough and it's like we don't even exist. I've been everywhere in the world, seen everything, had everything a man can have. Don't none of it mean nothin'." His tone is not cynical.

He shuffles awkwardly back to the sofa and drops heavily into his seat. "The only thing that matters is submitting to the will of God," he says. "The only things you've got is what's been given to you."

He gestures for me to join him by patting the cushion to his left. I take a seat. We touch knees and shoulders. Lonnie has taken a seat in a chair across from us and beside the TV.

"How you been?" Ali asks.

"I'm okay," I say, "but my dad died a few months ago."

The Champ jerks his head up, surprised.

"My father just died, too," Lonnie says.

Ali turns and looks at me so empathetically you'd think we shared the same parentage. "How old was he?" he asks.

"Only fifty-nine. And I thought he was healthy. I thought I'd have lots of time with him. He was both my father and my mother. It's the hardest thing I've ever been through."

"How'd he pass?" Lonnie asks.

"A heart attack?" says Ali.

I nod yes.

"My father, too," Lonnie says with a note of connection to my loss, as well as the raw recognition of her own.

"I'm sorry, Lonnie," I say, nodding.

Ali pats me on the hand. "I know you miss him. When I first won the title, people used to call me up, messin' with me, tell me my father'd been killed. Used to scare me so bad. Life is so, so short. Bible says it's like a vapor."

Ali picks up the TV's remote control from the sofa's armrest and tours the channels. Lonnie gets up, her eyes tearing. "You two visit while I change clothes," she says and leaves the room.

Ali stops on a music network that's playing an old Michael Jackson hit. He turns off the sound; we watch.

"Gandhi," he says as the Indian spiritualist's gray ghostlike image flashes onto the screen. "Mother Teresa," a few seconds later. It's obvious that he feels a kinship with the faces and their deeds and wants me to recognize the connection. He intones the names as if they were incantations.

When the song is over, he switches to a segment of a workout show. Young chesty women stylishly sweat in blue and pink and yellow Easter-egg-colored leotards. "They call this exercisin'," Ali says. "This is what it's really about." He places his left hand near his lap and simulates the common male masturbatory technique. "It's hard not to be tempted by this, unless you got somethin' like I got, somethin' holy."

He leans around the corner and looks down the hall to where Lonnie disappeared. "Haven't fucked around in almost five years," he says, low and secretive. "The last time, a brother in Saudi Arabia caught me with a woman. Asked, 'Would you do that in front of your mother?' I told him, 'No.' He pointed at me and said, 'You're doin' it in front of your Father, doin' it in front of Allah.' *Maaann*, that's heavy. Powerful. He scared me. That's when I really began to get serious about livin' for God."

He uses his right arm to reach across the chrome and glass coffee table. "Want to show you somethin'," he says. When I last saw Ali, his left hand trembled. The right one did not; now it does.

He grabs his briefcase, which lies on the floor in front of us. He places it on his knees and opens it slowly, reverentially, as if revealing the contents of the Ark of the Covenant. When I see inside, I'm reminded of Gandhi's possessions at his time of death—one pair of eyeglasses, a watch, two pair of sandals, an eating bowl, a *Bhagavad-gita*. Ali's briefcase contains thick stacks of yellow, green, and blue Muslim pamphlets, his own eyeglasses, a photo of himself with Sugar Ray Robinson on the left and Joe Louis on the right, a Koran, a Bible. He removes a painting of a profile of Jesus's face and white-cloaked shoulders, which he holds up, widening his eyes like he used to when challenging an opponent or a group of reporters.

"I carry this everywhere I go. It reminds me just how famous I am. If you had your whole life handed back to you right now, and your one goal, from the moment you were born, was to become famous as this man, how would you do it? If somebody told you some nigger boxer from Loovul, Kentucky, would become famous as Jesus Christ, you'd tell 'em, 'You crazy.' But I did it."

I don't expect to run into Jesus at a gas station or on a street corner, but this big-as-Christ talk makes me uncomfortable for Ali. "Did you?" I ask. "Or was it done for you?"

He grins and laughs like my four-year-old caught with a stick of candy he has been asked not to eat. "You got me there," he says. And then he drapes a bear's arm about my shoulders. "I still get arrogant sometimes. You really straightened me out."

Ali growls his growl and bites his lower lip. Then, with his thumb and index finger, he grabs my right leg just above the knee and sort of pinches it in a rolling, tickling way. Giggling, I knock his hand to the side. This is the first time I think I've laughed since my dad died. Leave it to Ali to help me feel better. I say: "Did I ever tell you I lost my virginity during the third Norton fight?"

"You serious?"

"Yeah, man. I was at my father's house with my girlfriend. Nobody was home. We're in my bedroom and we've been there for a while. All of a sudden, my dad opens the back door. We hadn't heard his car drive up. Lyn jumps out of bed and runs bare-ass for the bathroom, clothes in hand. I flip on the TV, vault into a pair of gym shorts, and try to act like I'm absorbed in the fight. I'll tell you the truth, I couldn't even see what was going on. My dad comes into the room and I'm trying so hard to be calm I'm shaking everywhere, shaking all over, shaking like I've been pureed in a blender. I know he knew exactly what was going on, but he never said a thing."

Ali laughs a long time, stamping his feet on the floor. As he wipes his eyes, he says, "Your father was a good man."

He returns his briefcase to the floor, moves for the bathroom, and when he gets there, slowly takes a starched white shirt from its hanger on the door and slips it on, then struggles a little with the buttons. Without tucking the shirt in his trousers, he pulls a royal-red tie over his head that has been pre-knotted, I'm sure, by Lonnie. He looks at me through the mirror and nods slightly, which I take to mean he'd like my help. In this moment, the most gifted athlete of the twentieth century looks so eggshell fragile I find *my* hands shaking a little. I might have imagined performing this service for my dad, had he lived to his seventies. Never for Muhammad Ali.

Ali is so large I have to stand on my toes to reach over and across the huge expanse of his back to slip the tie under his collar. He tucks his shirt in his trousers without unsnapping or unzipping, and then tugs on his jacket. Without being asked, I pick a few motes of white lint from the jacket's dark surface and help him straighten his tie. He grabs cookies and an apple from the glass dining table and points to his briefcase. I pick it up. We head for the door.

I shout down the hall, saying goodbye to Lonnie. "It's good to see you, Davy," she yells.

In the elevator, Ali leans to me and whispers, "All these people gamblin'. It's important to come to people where they are. Watch how people react."

When we reach the ground floor, he crams cookies in his jacket pocket, pushing the flap halfway down inside, then places the apple core in an ashtray, takes his briefcase from my hand, and, as the elevator doors open, loudly clucks his tongue across the roof of his mouth. The sound is almost instantaneously repeated from probably twenty feet away. Within seconds, a face appears in the doorway. It's Howard Bingham, Ali's personal photographer and best friend for nearly thirty years. Bingham looks basically the way I recall from the

1970s: angular, awkward, balding, bearded, and hang-jawed like the 1950s MGM cartoon character Droopy.

I introduce myself to Bingham and we walk from the elevator, Ali in the lead, Bingham behind me. We don't get more than fifteen steps before probably one hundred people surround us, wanting to touch Ali or shake his hand. Cameras appear from women's purses, as do pens and scraps of paper. "Do the shuffle, Champ," an older man shouts.

Ali hands me his briefcase, gets up on his toes, and dances to his left. He tosses a few slow jabs at several people, then for a couple of seconds urges his feet to blur into the patented Ali shuffle. The crowd, ever growing, explodes into laughter and applause. A space clears behind him and he uses it, knows it's there without turning to look. He walks backward, moving toward the far corner of the wide hallway, waving his audience forward, then turns to take his briefcase from me. Bingham reappears with a metal folding chair. Ali sits, places the briefcase on his lap and produces a cheap ballpoint pen from the pocket of his jacket.

Two minutes later, there is no way to skirt the throbbing crowd around Ali. There's every bit of five hundred people in the hallway. A Mirage security guard uses his walkie-talkie to call for reinforcements and directs people who want autographs into a line.

I stand at Ali's right shoulder, against the wall. Bingham is to my left. We're in those exact positions for nearly an hour before I ask Bingham, "Is it always like this?"

"Always," he says. "Everywhere in the world. Last year, over two hundred thousand came to see him in Jakarta."

"How long will he do this?" I want to know, meaning today.

Bingham shrugs. "Until he gets tired. For hours. All day."

Ali gives nearly every waiting person something personal. He talks to almost no one, yet most everyone seems to understand what he means. He gestures with his hands, fingers, head, eyes. He signs each person's first name on the Muslim literature and hugs, and is hugged by, three-year-old tykes and their eighty-year-plus great-grandmamas. Whenever kids are near, he goes out of his way to pick them up and snuggle and kiss them, sometimes more tenderly than one might imagine their own parents doing. The first time I met him, one of the first questions he asked was if I had kids. I now want to know why he connects so to children.

"They're angels in exile," he replies, looking at me over his shoulder and speaking in the same tone you'd expect from a monk exposing the uninitiated to the mysteries. "Children are so close to God. They haven't had time to separate from Him."

Women and men in line openly weep upon seeing Ali. Many recount stories about his impact on their lives. Some tell of having met him years before. He often pretends to remember. "You was wearin' a brown suit," he jokes with men. "You was in a blue suit," he tells women.

A huge, rough, Italian-American fellow in his mid-forties takes Ali's hand, kisses it, and waves away an autograph. "I don't want anything from you, Champ," he says. His mud-brown eyes are red and swollen. "We've taken too much already." I feel a need to touch Ali's shoulder. When I do, I'm sure he notices, but he doesn't react.

I stay with Ali for a couple of hours, but eventually I have to leave to do a couple of radio and television interviews my editor has scheduled for me. Several times during the day, I pass Ali and Howard on the way to or from my room. Until late at night, Ali is signing and hugging and kissing and posing for photographs. There's always a line waiting for him that stretches around the corner and out of sight.

✦   ✦   ✦   ✦

I HAVE BREAKFAST with Ali and Lonnie the next morning. He's wearing the same suit and tie. Even when he was fighting, and making tens of millions of dollars, he didn't own a lot of clothes at any one time. He's seldom worn jewelry and his watch is a Timex.

I ask why, unlike the old days, everyone, everywhere, seems to love him. "Because I'm *baadd*," he clowns, but then holds up his shaking left hand, spreads its fingers, and says, "It's because of this. I'm more human now. It's the God in people that connects them to me."

Two

ALI'S FATHER DIES of heart disease. When I get the news,
I call his mom's house to give my condolences. Lonnie answers the
phone.

"How's he taking it?" I ask.

"Better than I thought he would," she answers.

I ask to speak with Mrs. Clay, who tells me, "Even fifty years ago,
my husband always said he'd die at seventy-seven. I guess he was
right. He lived a full life."

I don't talk to The Champ. I ask Mrs. Clay to say hello for me.

Ali and Cash.

Three

IN MIAMI INTERNATIONAL AIRPORT, I unexpectedly run into Ali. As usual, he's at the center of a crowd and people are looking at him with the same sweet sadness they usually reserve for a favorite uncle who has recently suffered a stroke.

As always, he's not surprised to see me. He's wearing a black short-sleeve shirt, a pair of black dress trousers. He's carrying about a hundred of his Muslim handouts. His hair needs combing and his face is puffy; he looks exhausted.

"Been to see Angelo Dundee," he tells me. "Been travelin' too much. I'm tired of travelin'. Before this, I was in Saudi Arabia. It's too Western—a holy place they've made so American. They care too much about money and possessions."

I ask if he'd like a root beer. We walk a couple of hundred yards to a coffee shop. A few people follow along until we go inside.

As we enter, he spots a woman with her head folded into her arms, slumped across a table. He takes a seat beside her and asks what's wrong. She looks up and doesn't seem to recognize Ali, but tells him that her purse has been stolen. The woman is short and dumpy, and she's wearing a pink warm-up suit. She has graying black hair and deep-set green eyes that bulge as if someone has grabbed her around the neck and squeezed, not real hard, but steadily for many, many years.

She laughs wearily. "It had all my money in it. I don't know how I'm going to get home. And how can I tell my husband? He doesn't like me spending so much, anyways. Sometimes we have some real blowouts over money."

Ali puts his pamphlets on the table and pulls a tattered brown cowhide wallet from his trousers pocket. It has $300 in cash in it and an old picture of him with all eight of his kids. Although he's no longer world-class wealthy, he gives the woman $280.

Four

AUGUST 1990

THE CHAMP GREETS ME AT THE DOOR to his mother's house in Louisville. It's very hot today, over 100. He's wearing a sky-blue seersucker safari suit and the same pair of white sneakers he was wearing the afternoon I first met him in 1988. His face has lost much of its puffiness; his pecan-colored skin refracts the late summer sun. In this moment, he looks much like the Ali we all remember. "My man," he says.

"You look good," I tell him. "How much weight you lost?"

"Can you really tell?" he asks, sounding flattered. "I'm down to two-twenty-four." That's the least he's weighed since 1980. In the final years of his career, he fought in the mid-220s. "Goin' all the way to two-ten. Won't eat nothin' but chicken and fish, fruit and vegetables. No grease. Drink lots of water." His voice seems different, a bit stronger. When he speaks, there's no longer a wet sound in his throat.

"You're starting to look pretty again. Are you working out?"

"I'm trainin'. Started by walking twenty-five miles a day. I'm not walkin' no more. Doin' five rounds heavy bag, five speed bag, five shadowboxin'."

I step into the foyer. "I'm trainin' for a spiritual battle," he says as he closes the door behind me.

It is four weeks since Iraq invaded Kuwait. Forces of Western nations are massing at the Saudi Arabian border. This morning on NPR's *Morning Edition*, a commentator said that there may soon be half a million American troops in the area.

I follow Ali to the kitchen. He pulls a quart bottle of mineral water from the refrigerator and downs a third of it in one bubbling gulp. I take a chair at a cream-colored, chrome-trimmed dinette table. Cassius Clay Sr.'s stained and yellowed registration card for a 1972 convertible Cadillac is propped between salt and pepper shakers. The room is hot and musty. I pick up the paper and think about my father's Social Security card sitting on my desk at home.

"How do you feel?" I ask.

"Got more energy. Move better."

Mrs. Clay comes into the room. "Oh, I'm so glad you're here," she says to me. She's wearing a yellow paisley dress and she smells of flour. Although she seems tired and a light sweat shines on her forehead and neck, she smiles her invariably fragile smile. "Would you like a glass of root beer?" she asks.

She brings the soda in an old Welch's jelly glass. Ali leaves the room to go upstairs for his midday prayers.

"Doesn't he look better?" she says, sounding hopeful. "I told you he did. He looks so young. It makes him feel he can fight again. He couldn't do that, could he?"

"No," I say. "No one would let him."

She looks relieved. "Before the Foreman fight," she says, "everybody was so nervous, thought he'd lose, maybe even get hurt. He told me he'd win, but he was the only one who was sure. In the corner, when he was praying, I saw bright lights all around him and knew he would win.

"Now, he doesn't talk anymore. He's so quiet you forget he's in the house. He reads and writes, writes and reads all the time."

Ali returns to the kitchen, still barefoot from his prayers, moving so quietly I can't help but believe he's trying not to disturb even the dust beneath his feet. We go downstairs and sit side by side on the sofa. As usual, he flips on the television. An MC Hammer music video is playing. He studies the bodies jumping across the screen and says, "Looks foolish. What do you think?"

I think so, too.

"Black folks always foolin' themselves," he says. "Need somebody so bad, they turn anybody into a hero. Pimps, pushers, a drug-usin' mayor, any kind of crook. It don't matter who."

A gold-framed certificate I haven't seen before is hanging crooked above the TV. I get up to see what's on it.

"In Memoriam," it reads, "the Los Angeles County Board of Supervisors extends its deepest sympathy to you in the passing of your beloved father, Cassius Marcellus Clay, in whose memory all members adjourned in tribute and reverence at its meeting of February 13, 1990."

I straighten the plaque.

"It was a relief," Ali says before I have a chance to ask. "He was gettin' so old, in so much pain all the time. Talked to him a week before he died. He said he wouldn't see me again. 'I'm tired,' he said. 'Tired of this pacemaker. Don't want it no more.' It happens to all of us. It'll happen to me before long, it'll happen to you. We all get tired. We'll close our eyes and won't open them again. I'm preparing myself for the next life. That's what matters now."

The phone rings. He answers. "They'll be killin' Muslims," he says into the receiver. "Killin' each other. Don't want that to happen."

He's on the phone about fifteen minutes—a long time for Ali. He talks some, but mostly listens. The male voice on the other end is loud, deep, persistent.

As he hangs up, he tells me, "I'm glad you're here. I need some advice." The look on his face is serious.

"People want me to go to Iraq and Saudi Arabia," he says. "Stand between two big armies gettin' ready to fight. They want me to put up my arms and say, 'I'm Muhammad Ali. Don't shoot.' They believe I can stop the war. Do you think I should do it?"

"Well . . . I don't know. It's not something I'd do." I want to be gentle, but would like to discourage him.

He appears to drop the subject and leaves the room. Mrs. Clay brings lunch. Canned-tuna sandwiches on white bread, canned peaches and pears. Ali returns with a portable cassette player I'd given him the last time I saw him. He's playing a sermon. He has dozens of Muslim lectures and messages, but until I offered him the recorder I'd been using to tape interviews for my articles, he apparently had nothing on which to play them when he was traveling. The speaker's voice sounds warbled. The batteries are losing power; I'm sure he won't replace them when they go dead. We eat slowly, without talking, as Ali listens to the sermon. When he's through eating, he pushes the stop button and turns to me.

"The one thing I'll never understand is war," he says, sounding genuinely puzzled. And, ten seconds later, looking at me deep: "Why have you followed me so long?" he asks, curious and surprised. I feel the full weight of him as he watches me.

"It's because you're the largest person I've ever seen," I say, "the single largest person I can imagine." I don't mean so much his physical size; I'm considering how, for these many decades, Ali has readily harbored opposing ideas, how he has been so many different people, often in the very same moment.

He nods, understanding me. "I've traveled the whole world," he says. "Learn somethin' from people everywhere. Watch children and see myself not long ago. See old folks and know it's even less time before I'm one of them. Then I think, 'I already *am* one of them.'

There ain't no differences between us. There's truth in Hinduism, Christianity, Islam, Buddhism, all religions. And in just plain talkin'. The only religion that matters is the real religion—love."

Ali and I return to the sofa. I think about the mystic poet Rumi, how much the present-day Ali, the Ali I'm friends with, has in common with Rumi's love-is-all Islamic Sufism. And I find myself remembering this Rumi line: "There is nothing in the universe that you are not."

I ask about Ali's prayers; he shows me a book that details the way for Muslims to pray.

He says, "I'm tired. I need a nap. The heat's botherin' me." The words sound ancient, totemic. "Are you gowna be here when I wake up?" he asks.

"I think I'll go on home," I tell him. "I have work to do."

He reaches to hug me, all the while watching my eyes. His body is so thick, his skin cool and moist through the thin shirt. I remember rubbing my dad's back and shoulders in the hospital. Next Tuesday, it'll be exactly one year since he died. Ali's skin smells of earth and of trees. I kiss him on the cheek.

"Be cool and look out for the ladies," he says, his standard way of saying goodbye.

Interlude:
Desert Storm

IN NOVEMBER, ALI TRAVELS TO BAGHDAD to meet with Saddam Hussein and make a plea for peace.

Unbeknownst to him, two of his traveling partners, an attorney named Arthur Morrison and Ali's longtime manager, Herbert Muhammad, try to make a few hundred thousand Euro-dollars for themselves by transporting a boxing ring to an area near Saudi Arabia's border with Kuwait and coercing Ali into fighting a ten-round exhibition. When Lonnie Ali finds out, Morrison's association with The Champ is abruptly concluded. Eventually, Herbert Muhammad becomes unwelcome around Ali. At the end of his ten-day mission, Ali returns to New York with fifteen Americans who had been held hostage by the Iraqi regime.

The Zen of Muhammad Ali: Part Two

One

APRIL 1991

I'M IN PHILADELPHIA FOR A DINNER that will mark the twentieth anniversary of the first Ali–Frazier fight. This morning, Ali has been at Frazier's gym, signing autographs for children (and for anyone else who wants one). He quit training during his stay in Iraq and has gained a lot of weight. He's at probably two-fifty, but as always, he is standing erect against the burden of gravity.

Frazier is agitatedly prowling his upstairs office. I stop by to introduce myself, say that I'm the boxing editor at *Sport* magazine and that I grew up watching his fights. "You're one of the all-time best," I say, serious about the compliment. He pays zero attention to me, staring instead at a dirty yellow naugahyde loveseat behind me. I ask if he'll autograph a photo from the Wilfrid Sheed biography that Ali had inscribed the evening I first met him in Louisville. I open the book to a picture of Frazier and Ali glaring at one another through a chicken-wired glass window. "Ten thousand dollars" are the only words and effort Frazier affords me.

As Ali and I leave the Frazier gym, I slide into the limo and take a seat directly across from him. An almost skeleton-thin elderly man startlingly appears beside the limousine, tapping on my window with his left knuckles. I jump. "Mr. Clay, Mr. Clay," he shouts, the sound of rotted teeth in his voice as he offers Ali, who never eats pork, a hot dog. The man is stubble-cheeked and his eyes are yellow with age, cheap wine, and a life spent on street corners.

Ali motions me to lower my window. He takes the old guy's hand for a moment.

As we leave the curb, I ask, "Do you let everybody in?" I've never seen him refuse anyone.

"I'm glad people care about me. It's a blessing. Don't want to disappoint nobody. But there's a lot of people who hurt you without meanin' to."

One thing I want everyone to understand who's reading this: the only thing that's special about my relationship with Ali is that it's mine. He treats almost everyone exactly the way he treats me. This is part of what's extraordinary about him. It's hard to imagine that there has ever been anyone else quite like Ali, and it's doubtful that there ever will be again.

We pull up to a stoplight. To my left, a heavy woman, dressed in layer upon layer of rags in shades of brown and gray and who has no legs or hands, is propped against a doorway. She is playing "Amazing Grace" on a harmonica that has been attached to her mouth by a strand of what looks to be white plastic clothesline. "We don't know how that lady got here," Ali says. "She's just like you and me." As he says this, his left hand begins to dramatically tremble. We near the Hotel Atop the Bellevue, where we're staying. Ali closes his eyes, drops into a light sleep, and begins to snore.

One of the first things one notices when spending serious time with Ali is that his life remains larger than that of anyone almost any of us has known, and that he seems less than fulfilled only when we see him in the smallest of ways, when we don't recognize that his Parkinson's disease and its attendant aura of silence extends his legend, enlarges the seeming meaning of his life. In a way, his silence helps him come off as something of a seer, a whispering muse. As his health is deteriorating, he's becoming a more spiritual being. Most of the time, he no longer aches with the ambition and the violence of a young god; some of his ego has thankfully been washed away.

I study the shape of his head, watch its almost perfect symmetry. He looks like a sleeping newborn, or a Buddha. Maybe he's some kind of bodhisattva. And maybe Ali is also a little like Chance, the gardener, in Jerzy Kosinski's novel *Being There*—a slate onto which we write what we wish, a screen onto which almost anything can be projected.

✦　✦　✦　✦

AS ALI AND I step from the limo in front of the Hotel Atop the Bellevue, he's greeted by a crowd of several hundred people on the sidewalk and spilling over onto the street.

Near the outside of this group, an Asian man in his mid-thirties places his young son on his shoulders so he can get a clean look at The Champ. "That's the greatest man in the world," he says to his boy in a rolling Southern accent. When the man is able to make it to Ali, he asks for an autograph for his son and tells Ali that they have come to see him all the way from their home in Arkansas. Stepping away, I walk along the fringe of this troop and enter the hotel.

The Ali family is congregating in the lobby. There's Bingham and Ali's daughters Miya and May May, who looks a little like Janet Jackson. Mrs. Clay is sitting in a high wingback chair. "Oh, I didn't know you'd be here," she says. "I'm so happy to see you." She's lost a few pounds and looks even more fragile than usual. She's recently suffered a stroke and isn't recovering well.

Lonnie is standing beside Mrs. Clay. She has an oversized blue canvas bag slung over her right shoulder and a quite young infant in her arms. "Hi, Lonnie," I say. "Whose baby?"

"He's ours," she says, and laughs because I'm stunned by this news. "Doesn't he look like Muhammad?"

She lowers the baby where I can have a peek. The baby's skin is nearly an identical copper color to her husband's. "He does look like Muhammad," I say. "What's his name?"

"Ask Muhammad," she says, frowning. "He says he's going to name the baby, but you know Muhammad—he can't make up his mind. He wants to call him Ahad, which means 'the one and only.' I keep telling him that's not the right name for a Muslim baby."

"How old is he?"

"He'll be one month tomorrow," she answers.

I step back and take a quick look. Her face is maybe a little drawn, but she doesn't seem like she's had a child within the past few weeks. "We're adopting him," she explains. "We're waiting for the papers to come from Louisville."

As Ali makes it to the lobby, he reaches for his new son, pulling the baby to his face, kissing him and then holding him to his right cheek with a tenderness that almost makes me want to turn away. In this moment, Ali looks as pleased as anyone I've ever seen.

"Didn't get to see the other eight growin' up," the proud papa says with profundity. "I'm gowna enjoy this baby."

"It's good to have something new in your life," I say, "something that's growing."

"Want to have five more," he tells me. "All races. When I'm seventy-five years old, they'll be twenty."

"Are you serious?" I ask, although this melds into his mythology— Muhammad Ali the international man, the champion granddaddy of the whole wide world.

"Naw, it's just a dream," he says. "I know it's a dream."

✦   ✦   ✦   ✦

WE'RE SITTING at the dining table in the Ali suite. Ali is trying to feed his son from a bottle while Lonnie orders room service. The boy's head is at the wrong angle, and despite having fathered at least eight kids by at least four mothers, the old fighter isn't experienced enough at the feeding ritual to recognize he's doing this all wrong. He pours milk all down the baby's face.

Lonnie hurries from across the room. "Muhammad, let me have that child before you drown him," she scolds.

While waiting on lunch, Lonnie suggests a name: Asaad Amin Ali. "It means 'son of the lion,'" she says. It would be tough to imagine a more perfect moniker.

Her husband nods his approval.

✦   ✦   ✦   ✦

THROUGHOUT THE DAY, a near-constant processional flows in and out of the Ali suite. Philadelphia-area Muslims offer Southern-style, stewed-vegetable dinners and sweet bean pies; a fellow who makes Muhammad Ali chocolate chip cookies and potato chips brings samples, of which Ali himself munches bag after bag; Ali intimates I recognize from TV screens joke and kid and hug The Champ. Baby Asaad is regularly brought out of the bedroom and is shown around. Ali is chuckling and smiling and sneaking up behind people, making cricket noises with his fingers. Rahaman gets in from Louisville. He, Bingham, and Ali shove and clinch and wrestle around the room while Mrs. Clay watches. Ali backs Bingham into a corner with goofy, looping punches. Bingham kicks toward Ali's groin to get him to back off. "He knows better than to mess with me," Ali's best friend tells me. "I ain't afraid of him. He knows it'll cost him."

"Just like the old days," Mrs. Clay says to me. "Nothing's changed a bit."

Rahaman tells Lonnie that he doesn't have a place to stay and that the hotel is sold out. I offer to let him room with me. Rock finds this idea hilarious. "Little buddy," he says, laughing and hissing and bending over and covering his face with his hands. But he takes me up on my offer.

Over fifteen hundred persons have paid $250 per plate for the privilege of eating dinner in the same room with Ali and Frazier. In the big anteroom, a much larger tide, maybe three thousand, laps up against the Ali island as we make our way toward the ballroom. As Ali enters the room, the old primal chant goes up: *"Ahh-lee! Ahh-lee! Ahh-lee!"*

Before he allows himself to be seated, he walks over to Frazier and attempts to kiss his old foe on the cheek. Frazier leans away from Ali's attentions and glares a hard man's glare and brilliantly cold smile: a teeth-exposed, stuck-tight steel zipper on a January morning in northern Alaska.

Ali's chair is on the right side of the dais, Frazier's is on the left. Frazier gets up to make a speech. "Twenty years later, he's still tryin' to start somethin'," he says, glowering. "He got himself in trouble to begin with because he wouldn't let me say nothin'. Now, when I'm talkin', he comes up behind me, makin' a noise like he's stickin' a bug or somethin' in my ear. He can't even talk no more, but he's always tryin' to make noise. Always messin' with me."

Frazier chooses not to get over having been called an Uncle Tom and a gorilla and generally having been treated as an inferior by the 1975 Ali, whose ego after knocking out Foreman was at its most monstrous. "I still want to take him apart piece by piece and send him back to Jesus," Frazier has said. Publicly and among his inti-mates, Ali says that he knows he was arrogant, cruel, and out of control, that he loves Joe Frazier, he's sorry that he hurt him, and wishes that Joe would forgive him.

May May steps up to the platform and drapes her arms about her dad. She whispers in his ear. He turns and smiles that easiest of smiles for her, the one we all remember. And then he laughs. He's having a good time.

She returns to her seat at the Ali family table, which is right beside mine. I look at Lonnie and the baby, Miya and May May, Mrs. Clay and smiling Rahaman, and wonder, with Mrs. Clay's health being as tenuous as it is, if this group will ever again appear together in public.

Ali picks up a piece of bread and begins to eat. He's the one person on the dais doing so, but he's not self-conscious. Throughout the speakers' introductions and the opening invocation by a Christian minister (this is, after all, Frazier's celebration for his own victory), Ali continues to chomp away. When he finishes the bread, he gets up from his seat, reaches behind the podium, and pulls a stack of tracts from his briefcase, which he begins to sign. He stops only when the lights have been dimmed and Frazier's son Marvis tells us that we'll be viewing highlights from the 1971 fight between his dad and Ali, the Fight of the Century. On the screen, Ali is wearing red velvet trunks; Frazier's are an iridescent green silk—exact opposites on the color wheel—and you can still feel the heat between these two come shimmering off of the screen. Ali has covered his eyes with his right hand. He is asleep and snoring.

Two

IT IS THREE WEEKS AFTER Ali's fiftieth birthday, and my fortieth. My six-year-old son, Isaac, is with me. He's never met The Champ, and I've wanted him to.

No one knows we're coming. I wanted to call Ali at home to see if it was a good time for us to visit, but Lonnie changes numbers more often than nuclear weapons facilities switch security codes, and I don't have current numbers. Yet, although Ali has been traveling almost constantly, I'm confident that if we drive up now, we'll be able to get with him. Things have almost always worked out when it comes to connecting with Ali.

Isaac and I make it to the farm around dusk. The wrought-iron gates are locked and the big MUHAMMAD ALI FARMS sign has been removed. When Ali is home, I've never seen the gates closed.

A light snow is falling; behind the dark metal bars, it sparkles on the driveway. Isaac is more excited by the snow than about the opportunity of meeting Ali. I step carefully from the car and push the small red button on the stainless steel intercom. To our right, a horse the color of hot chocolate is standing at a fence, shaking snow from its mane.

Lonnie's brother Mike answers on the fifth ring. After I explain who I am and what I hope will happen, he says, "They're not here. They haven't been home since Christmas and I don't expect them for two to three weeks."

I tell Mike I have videocassettes of a few of Muhammad's fights and interviews that I'd promised to mail to Lonnie. "Bring them on down," he says. "I'll open the gate."

Mike opens the door to the kitchen. I hand him the tapes and copies of a piece I'd written for the *Louisville Courier-Journal* and the *Los Angeles Times* for The Champ's fiftieth. As Isaac and I turn to leave for the long drive home, the phone rings. Mike answers in the adjoining den.

While he's out of the room, I tell Isaac, "I'm sorry you didn't get to meet Ali, but we've had a good time driving up and we'll have a good time on the way home."

Mike comes back to the kitchen. "Man, you're lucky," he says. "That was Lonnie. They'll get in late tonight. She said for you to come by first thing tomorrow."

✦   ✦   ✦   ✦

LONNIE OPENS the back door, carrying ten-month-old Asaad, whose hair is in a topknot, almost Japanese style. Asaad is large for his age. He has been walking since he was six months old, and Lonnie tells me that he weighs over thirty pounds. Asaad sees Isaac and struggles to get down. Isaac, who's usually uncomfortable around babies, is surprisingly attracted to Asaad; he playfully pulls on the toddler's foot and tweaks his stomach.

"Muhammad will want to meet you," I tell him. "Then you can play."

I've driven Isaac one thousand miles for this next moment, and I'm anxious to see it.

We step through the kitchen and into the family room. To our right, in the far corner, Ali is sitting at his desk, signing pamphlets. Three full, open black suitcases are at his feet. He's barefoot and not wearing a shirt; he's nearly as round as old Bodhidharma himself.

Ali looks at me and nods, almost invisibly, then reaches his arms out to my son, who moves slowly, reverentially forward. Ali's arms encircle him. Isaac has never had a strange man hug him like this, but I can tell by his expression that with Ali he doesn't mind. Indeed, he is flattered; he's smiling proud, nice, self-assured. "You'll remember this when you're an old, old man," Ali says, both to me and to my son.

As he places Isaac on his knee, Ali nods toward me again. He wants to be certain I don't feel slighted. "Happy birthday, Champ," I say.

After Isaac hops down, Ali pulls a red flannel shirt and a pair of white athletic socks from a suitcase, tugs them on, slips into a pair of black dress shoes. He turns to Isaac, who's playing with one of Asaad's toy cars. "Stay here," Ali says with respectful authority. "We'll be back." He waves for me to follow.

We go outside, stepping across the driveway to the garage. The day glows phosphorescently; snow is falling in chunks the size of an infant's hands. We enter the garage through a side door and climb a set of stairs. At the top, we pass a big desk, turn right, and walk down a short hallway. He pulls open a door. An otherwise empty space, the size of a large master bedroom, is piled floor to ceiling with boxes and envelopes and packages. "This is the mail I don't have time to open," he says.

I grab the two pieces closest to my foot. The top one is covered with brightly colored stamps. "From Indonesia," the world soul says. I feel a videocassette inside. The other is a thick letter on onionskin paper; the return address is in Kansas.

"Yesterday, I was in Washington at the Pentagon. I'm always somewhere. Want you to help me," he says. "Feel bad not bein' able to write everybody."

This is not an overstatement. Nearly every day when he is home, Ali invests three to four hours in opening letters and writing replies. He seems to feel that it's part of his mission to contact every person on the planet.

"Want to get a 900 number, where people can call and get a message, where I can talk with them. You're my man. Want you to find out how to do it."

We walk back to his office. He points to a phone on the desk. "Can you call from here?" he says. "Find out somethin'?"

He motions me into his intricately carved chair. "If I can just get my voice straightened out," he continues, easing onto a smaller chair on the opposite side of the desk, "I want to do this."

"If you want, I'll help," I say. But there's something I'd like to know. "Last year, at the twentieth-anniversary dinner of the first Frazier fight, you got up to speak and ended up talking for probably ten minutes. You didn't slur or stammer, your volume was fine, you were funny, your timing was good."

It's true. He was terrific. And I've seen it on several occasions over the past few years, always when there are no TV cameras on him. "How do you do that?" I ask.

He doesn't tell me. I doubt he knows. Instead, he falls into his old pre-fight voice. "This is Muhammad Ali, The Greatest of All Times. I did what I set out to do. Whupped Sonny Liston, whupped Joe Frazier, George Foreman, whupped the United States draft board . . ."

After thirty seconds or so, he stops and rubs his left hand across his face in the way I do when I've just woken from a night's sleep. "See wh-wh-what you can find out," he asks, his voice gurgling like the river behind his property.

I make calls and get basic information about 900 numbers. As we leave the garage, headed for the house, Lonnie, Asaad, and Isaac meet us halfway.

"Saadie wanted to go with you, Muhammad," Lonnie says. She hands the child to her husband and looks at his slick-soled shoes. "Don't you dare drop that baby," she says. Her tone is wifely, concerned, not patronizing. She turns and goes back to the house.

With Ali and Asaad in the lead, we trudge around the driveway. Soon, Ali's son decides he wants down. Ali lowers him to the ground, holding his left hand, and tries to get him to walk. Asaad turns to look at Isaac; he intends to play. I ask Isaac to take Asaad's right hand so he'll go with his daddy. My boy does so in a way that replicates Ali's gentleness. I stay a few feet behind, watching the three of them shuffle along at a ten-month-old's pace. For many minutes, Ali, Asaad, and Isaac plod back and forth in a chain through the snow. The only sounds are those of wind in bare rattling branches of trees and of Ali's scuffling feet and, in the distance, of water tumbling over rocks. Just before we go back inside, I reach to brush melting snow from the children's hair and shoulders, and from Ali's.

Three

LONNIE AND ASAAD LEAVE for the grocery store. Ali, Isaac, and I park ourselves on the sofa and put on a videocassette of The Champ's fight with Chuck Wepner. There's no commentary on this version. On the huge stereo TV, you hear Angie Dundee and Bundini Brown yelling from the corner, Ali talking to Wepner, the punches as they connect, and Ali's feet as he springs around the canvas. It's almost the experience of attending the fight live. Although I'm aware that Ali is playing the Wepner bout for my entertainment, the old narcissist immediately becomes riveted by his own image. Watching him silently concentrate on the first three rounds, he seems ageless. That is, his youth, middle years, and old age—everyone he has been, and everyone he will be?—are all present on his features. As he intently, religiously studies his own history on the screen, his hands and head stop trembling. I ask what he's thinking.

"I forget how good I was, what I used to could do," he says.

During the fourth round, the phone rings. Ali answers and listens for a moment. "You don't have no business callin' here, disturbin' my peace," he says. "I'm retired. Want to be left alone. Don't care nothin' 'bout boxin'."

He cups his hand over the phone and looks slyly at me. "Famous boxin' promoter," he says. Then, into the phone: "You say it's important because it's important to you. It don't mean nothin' to me. Boxin's dyin'. I always said it'd die when I left. I ain't goin' to your fights. I'm aware of my condition—all those people around, me shakin', press writin' about how pitiful I am. Don't need it. Don't call here no more."

While he's talking, I notice a letter on the coffee table and see that it's from a well-known movie director. Ali spots me reading and hangs up the phone without saying anything else to the caller. He points at the letter. "Wants to give me three million dollars to sign my life away. Don't care nothin' 'bout the money. Don't mean nothin' to me. Wouldn't mind a movie bein' made, if it was a good movie, about what's important. He'd want to make it sensational—that ain't my way no more."

Although I'm sure my doubts are different from Ali's own concerns, it hardly seems possible that this particular director could subtly replicate even the most basic events of Ali's huge, seemingly contradictory life. "I'd hate to see you made into some kind of cartoon," I tell him.

"I'm fifty years old now," he says. "That doesn't seem possible. When they gowna leave me alone, when is all this gowna stop? I wanta take two years off, quit all this travelin'. Stay home with my wife and son."

I've heard him say this before, but within half an hour he'll have me drive him to a shopping mall so he can sign autographs for two to three hours at a time. I get ready to tell him the obvious—that he'll never be left alone and he wouldn't like it if he were—but then Lonnie and Asaad come in from the store and I don't say anything.

She steps into the den with a pack of Bubblicious bubble gum, which she hands to Isaac. Asaad is wanting a piece for himself. "You're too young, Saadie," she says.

Ali widens his eyes. "How about me?" he asks.

To me, she says, "Muhammad can't keep gum out of his mouth. Go look under his desk."

I get up from the sofa, walk across the room, lean low, take a peek. Sure enough, there are dozens of fat pink wads all rammed up under The Great Man's formal mahogany desk.

I look across at him and begin to laugh; he's staring at me with a guilty grin that's in no way an affectation. "I know why you think it's funny," he says. "You have gum underneath your desk, too."

For lunch, Lonnie broils turkey burgers for Ali and me and makes a cheese sandwich for Isaac. She brings the food on metal lunch trays. "Here, Punkin," she says as she places Ali's tray in his lap.

Yes! "Punkin." How could any nickname be more perfect? His Southernness, the playfulness, his squnchability, his roundness. Even Ali's skin is the color of pumpkin pie.

On the same plate as his burger, Muhammad has three prescription pills: a red one, a blue one, an orange one. And a piece of pink bubble gum.

Four

ISAAC AND I STAY AT THE FARM for two days. Ali plays with my son hour upon hour, doing magic tricks, scaring and enchanting him with ghost stories ("I'm Frankenstein," says the king of all children. "I'm the Mummy. I'm gowna eat you up"), chasing him around the house, hiding behind furniture, jumping out to tickle him.

"When I was thirty," Ali confides, "I used to wonder when I was gowna quit playin'. Used to sorta worry about it. Now, I know I'm never gowna quit." When he isn't entertaining Isaac or talking with me, he's often asleep and snoring.

As we're leaving for our long drive home, he walks us to the car. I turn the key in the ignition while he closes our doors and waves goodbye. As we pull out of the driveway, Isaac is sitting in the back of the car, staring out the rear window. I ask my son if he is crying. He nods yes. I ask why. "He's so cool, I didn't think anybody could be that cool. I just wish he wasn't sick."

I tell him it's all right. And I honestly think that it is.

Five

ALI IS NOT THE FIRST PERSON to have suffered because of his art, his ego, his beliefs. "I'm more human now," he has regularly told me, pointedly spreading the fingers of his shaking left hand. "That's what makes so many people care. They believe I'm like them, and that's good."

All of us are changed by the work we do, Ali more noticeably than most of us. After all, he boxed more rounds than anyone else in history. Fight after fight. Exhibition after exhibition. Sparring session upon sparring session. Arena after arena. Gym after gym. Country upon country. City after city. Town after town. In backyards and on street corners. Just about any time someone produced a couple of pair of gloves. Long after he should have stopped. Oh, how he loved to box.

"A man goes to war," Ali says, "fights for his country, comes back with one leg. He either thinks it was worth it or wasn't. It's up to what he values. I look at my world fame, the people I've helped, the things I've done, spiritual and non-spiritual. I add it all up and I'd do it all over again."

Six

THE FOLLOWING WEEK, I go to Isaac's school to talk with his classmates about our visit to the farm. I ask the first-graders how many of them have heard of Muhammad Ali. It has been thirty years since that moonless night in Miami when he befuddled Sonny Liston; nearly twenty since he voodooed George Foreman in Zaire, two hours before the monsoons set in; almost as long since The Thrilla in Manila, when he whupped Joe Frazier (and his own health was dramatically damaged) in 115-degree heat. Indeed, it has been a very long while since he was the world's most beautiful and charismatic man, when he seemed to be constantly moving inside a singular and wondrous rhythm, when his eyes shone like radioactive chestnuts, when his skin glowed like fire witnessed through a copper-colored glass orb. Today. Now. All twenty-three six- and seven-year-olds raise their hands.

After I speak for a few minutes and answer questions, Isaac reads an Ali story he has written. We play a videotape that includes highlights from The Champ's career, as well as an Ali levitation scene we'd taped at the farm. At the end of class, kids erupt into the hallway shouting, "Float like a butterfly, sting like a bee" and "I'm a *baadd* man." Everybody, including the girls, throws punches at everybody else. The teachers look shocked. I'm sure I won't be invited back anytime soon.

For days thereafter, my son tells me, he reminds his classmates that they have seen a man named Muhammad Ali who can actually fly.

Interlude:
Jann Wenner

6 May, 1991

Mr. Jann Wenner, Editor-in-Chief
Rolling Stone
1290 Avenue of the Americas
New York, New York 10104

Dear Jann Wenner:

I enjoyed speaking with you yesterday; thank you for accepting my call. As I mentioned on the phone, I have a story idea that I believe will interest you. I'd like to write a 5,000 to 7,000 word piece that I would call "The Zen of Muhammad Ali." Access to the reclusive Ali is not a problem: I met him several years ago and ever since, he and I have been friends.

This friendship has allowed me to see much that is not widely recognized by the press, including not only that Ali's day-to-day life is considerably different from what has been reported, but that his worldwide popularity hasn't diminished since his retirement from boxing. Ali travels nearly 300 days of each year; throngs turn out to greet him wherever he goes, everywhere in the world.

In the years since the onset of Ali's Parkinson's disease, he has become intensely dedicated to a pursuit of the spiritual. "The Zen of Muhammad Ali" will propose a new Ali mythology, part of which is related to the idea of Ali as mystic, or, more precisely, as a vessel into which wisdom pours, and from which it flows, sometimes in ways that Ali himself doesn't recognize. On a recent visit to his mother's house in Louisville, Ali told me, "God's usin' me."

Intrigued, I asked him, "What's he using you for?"

"I don't know," he said. "And it don't matter if I know. What matters is He's doin' it, He's always done it."

In March of this year, over a quarter of a million people came to see Ali in Jerusalem. It's in no way an overstatement to say that Ali has tens of millions of fans. The basic reason that we don't see much about him in the press is that, these days, he doesn't want to be written about: a seeming paradox about Ali is that, although he is accessible to almost everyone on the street, everywhere, he feels that media coverage would violate the spiritual nature of his life.

In many ways, Ali exemplifies that which is classically Buddhist. Although there is a marked fragility about him, there is also that which seems eternal. He regularly sits on the edge of conversations, listening. The art of the gesture has become quite important for Ali. He communicates with his hands, his head, his eyes. He surprises visitors by making a sound with his fingers that's not unlike a cricket in your ear, he blows on the tops of heads, tickles the insides of palms as he shakes hands, does assorted prestidigitations: "Wake up, wake up," call these nontraditional koans. These qualities are (part of) the Zen of Muhammad Ali.

It goes without saying that Ali is not just another retired athlete: he is the most recognizable person of the twentieth century. People all over the globe admire Ali not only for the obvious reasons: the singular grace with which he fought for almost twenty-five years, his boastful prettiness, his huge charm and presence, his contagious, distinctive and childful humor, his brave stand against the Vietnam War (and all war), but also for the great, even noble dignity with which he has carried himself through his afflicted middle years.

My story will have nearly timeless and universal appeal. I'm not uncomfortable saying that it will be quite unlike anything that has ever been written about the world's most famous man. I look forward to soon hearing back from you and hopefully to working with you on this piece.

All best,
Davis Miller

Tokyo

"I HAVE AN IDEA FOR YOU," I tell my editor at *Sport*. "What about a piece called 'How to Beat Mike Tyson'?

"Everybody's talking this guy up," I continue, "making him sound indestructible. Just because he has a Nintendo game named after him doesn't mean he's superhuman. You wait and see—somebody's going to knock him off real soon."

"Okay," says my editor, "you've sold me. Let's do it. When's Tyson fighting next? We can run it before his next fight."

Truth is, I couldn't care less about Tyson. Our world heavyweight boxing champions have often mirrored the societies and years that spawned them. One thing I'll give Tyson is this: as hardworking, elegantly stoic Joe Louis was exactly the right champ for the Depression years of the 1930s and war-effort '40s, and ineffably bold, beautiful, and philosophic Ali was the ideal king for the expansive '60s and eclectic '70s, it's tough to imagine a more perfect world heavyweight champ than punk-chic, tree-trunk-thick Tyson for the "let's-grab-all-we-can" '80s, a decade when the abuse of extreme, even cartoonishly hypertrophic power has been greatly admired by far too many people. Tyson, whose less-than-one-round knockouts are perfectly suited for the attention spans of MTV-trained juvies. But I can't accept Tyson being favorably compared to Ali the way he has been recently in the press as well as on the street, and I don't want him threatening my man's rep in any way. Besides, I know what it takes to whup "Kong," as Ali privately calls the current heavyweight champion. It's obvious.

✦   ✦   ✦   ✦

"**MUCH OF WHAT** it will take to whip Tyson can be summarized simply," I write in my article. "It will take a tall, big fighter with a terrific chin, who has long arms and fast hands, who isn't afraid of Tyson, who stands up tall and uses his reach, and who will be close to a complete boxer.

"He'll show Tyson many rhythms, keep him confused with different looks. It's crucial that he remain always poised—alert, yet relaxed—in all these styles. He need not be as beautiful in movement as Muhammad Ali, but it's likely he will have studied films of Ali's fights, and may have idolized Ali."

The piece is published in the March issue of *Sport*, available on newsstands two weeks before Tyson's February 10, 1990, bout. I send a copy of the piece to Ali, with a note saying he might be interested in what I've written. I let him know that the fantasy Tyson conqueror whose attributes I describe is, of course, none other than The Greatest of All Times.

On February 10, I'm asleep in bed when my studio phone and the house line ring simultaneously a little before midnight.

Wondering what's wrong, I grope about the nightstand for the receiver. "He got knocked out!" Lyn's brother shouts in my ear. "They're counting over him right now!"

"Wh-what are you talking about?" I say, my mouth feeling like the pillow's still in it. "Who got knocked out?"

"Tyson! *Tyson* did!" says Scott. "He got knocked cold! He was down on the canvas, fumbling around for his mouthpiece!"

I jump from bed as if something important has happened. "Yes, yes, *yes!*" I shout into the receiver. "Lyn!" I yell, though she's lying right next to me. "Kong just got kayoed. Somebody knocked out Kong!"

"Who's 'Kong'?" my wife groggily asks.

"Scott, I'll call you tomorrow," I say. "I've got to go turn on the TV."

I buss Lyn on the cheek and fairly leap upstairs. The light is blinking on the answering machine, telling me I have a message. I turn off the ringer and the volume to the speaker and flip the TV to the sports channel. "Would you believe it?" a sculpted white-bread announcer is saying. "In the first heavyweight championship fight of the 1990s, journeyman fighter James 'Buster' Douglas has knocked out Mike Tyson to become the new heavyweight champion of the world."

On the screen, there are photos of Tyson's features getting reshaped by a long right hand, thrown Ali-style. Douglas looks to be about Ali's size; he's wearing Ali tassels on his shoes. And there's a shot of the new champ mugging for the camera while being interviewed in the ring, mouth open and fist cocked beside his head in the Ali manner.

✦   ✦   ✦   ✦

FOR A COUPLE HOURS, I rove from channel to channel, rejoicing in seeing Tyson get dumped flat on his proper place in ring history. I jump about the room, throwing jabs, stopping occasionally to whip out a combination or explode into the shuffle. I feel twenty-two years old. By the time I'm ready for bed, fourteen messages have come in on the answering machine. The first voice is my editor's. "Davis, this is Kelly. Congratulations. Give me a call first thing tomorrow."

The second message is also from someone I'm pretty sure I recognize: "They gowna compare Tyson to me now?" says the faceless caller, his voice sounding about as mighty as God's would be echoing off of the moon.

✦   ✦   ✦   ✦

BY THE TIME I get back with Kelly, *Sport* has received dozens of calls about my story. "We were getting them before the fight, too," he says, chuckling. "Nearly everybody was critical of the idea that Tyson could ever go down."

It's weird. On my answering machine, I've got messages from newspapers all around the country, and the *Winston-Salem Journal* is going to run a long piece about my Tyson article, as if I've actually accomplished something. I'm getting all this attention for the closest thing to non-writing I've ever done.

Kelly says that he wants me to write profiles of Douglas and the major heavyweight contenders, including old George Foreman, Evander Holyfield, and a follow-up Tyson piece. He'll publish an article every issue for the next six months and will pay two thousand dollars per story. "Man, I'm glad I made you the magazine's boxing editor. You've definitely earned your keep," he says.

I ask if this means I'll be placed on the payroll, if I'll have a salary.

"I wish it did," he says. "That's not the way this company does things. I can't even guarantee a minimum amount of money each year. But I'll keep trying to take care of you," he promises.

This'll bother Lyn some. She wants me to have a regular wage. But at least I can tell her I'll make a minimum of twelve thousand from writing this year. And that, with her job and the interest from what's left of Daddy's inheritance, should be enough. I tell Kelly yes, I'm happy too, but I don't tell him I'm not especially interested in boxing. I'm happy because these *Sport* magazine assignments give me time to develop my writing skills—and greater opportunity to regularly spend time with Ali.

Columbus, Ohio

THROUGH ALI'S INFLUENCE, folks have become jazz singers, dancers, basketballers, astronauts, environmental activists, standup comics, painters, chess champions, TV and movie producers and directors, high-wire artists; they have joined the Peace Corps, become conscientious objectors, and yes, have become kickboxers and writers. Ray Leonard became Sugar Ray; Bruce Lee regularly studied film of Ali fights and emulated Ali's patterns of movement to become Bruce Lee, the god of movie martial art; Jimmy Connors was the first Ali of tennis (tennis brats—and every other sports punk since—have unfortunately been in the Ali lineage); Nelson Mandela says he became Nelson Mandela partly because of being inspired by Ali.

"He was my hero," James "Buster" Douglas tells me when I'm in Columbus to interview him for *Sport*. We're tooling around in his restored metallic-green 1970 Coupe de Ville. Douglas's window is down, mine is up, his left foot is out the window, and on it is a size-fourteen blinding-red lizard-skin boot. His round, smooth-skinned, good-hearted worker's face shines. It's the face Sonny Liston would have had, had he been a kind man. Douglas and I are chewing on oatmeal and raisin cookies he bought at a gas station.

"As an amateur, I tried to do everything I saw Ali do," says Douglas. "Used to wear trunks like his, white with black stripes, still wear Ali tassels. Only *arteests* wear tassels. I learned a lot from Ali. Learned to be nice to people. Got to meet him in Huntington, West Virginia, last week. He went to dinner with me, told me how happy it made him that I won. He jumped two feet out of his chair with his hands over his head and said that's what he did when I knocked out Short Man."

I ask Douglas to sign a copy of my Tyson piece. "Man, I read this on the plane to Tokyo for the fight. Everybody in my corner was passin' this around the plane."

He takes a pen from my hand. "Mike Tyson Can Be Beat," reads the headline. Above the title, in bold blue letters, Douglas writes, "And I'm The Man That Done It."

The Reverend
Doesn't Play Fair . . .

NOVEMBER 1991

A FOUR-INCH-LONG LIZARD the color of southeast Texas dust scurries about the surface of a white sign with hand-painted olive lettering. The lizard is looking for a place to hide and it can't find one. It jumps nervously to the ground and scratches away into thin brown grass around a cluster of scraggly pines. The sign from which the lizard has leapt reads, CHURCH OF THE LORD JESUS CHRIST.

I'm in Houston on assignment for *Sport*. It's Sunday, almost 10 A.M. The Reverend George Edward Foreman is standing under an overhang beside the beige modular corrugated-metal building that functions as his sanctuary. Foreman looks as if he might have organically appeared out of the very ground around the church. Sweat runs in beaded rivulets down his forehead and the sides of his face. He's wearing a black vest that's too tight to button, a pair of almost matching trousers and a thin, inexpensive short-sleeve white shirt that can barely contain his arms and neck. The fabric is stretched almost to the ripping point. His right foot is propped on the second stair of the concrete steps that lead into the church. He welcomes his fold as they enter.

Inside, on a small platform, a long-faced, long-haired, thick-shouldered man in his thirties sits on a stool and strums a shining sunburst-patterned Gibson electric guitar while singing a happy-sounding hymn. Compared to the stark exterior, the comfort and attractiveness of the small room is surprising. The walls are the color of lime sherbet; two large arrangements of tiger lilies and white-and-purple orchids adorn opposite sides of the pulpit. There are six rows of well-maintained dark oak pews, enough seating for maybe seventy-five people, although there aren't one-third that many in attendance today (and the ones who are bear an unmistakably strong genetic resemblance to the reverend).

Throughout his sermon, Pastor Foreman howls and prowls, back and forth, up and down, his tone sounding like a poor man's Ali. He warns not to take that drink on Saturday night and not to lay with that inviting stranger. "Some people don't even believe in a supernatural God," he shouts near the end of his message. "I wouldn't serve a god who wouldn't speak to me. I was talkin' to a fella one time and he told me he turned toward somewhere and prayed eight or nine times a day. And he showed me how he put his head down to the ground. I said, 'Man, does God ever speak to you?' He said, 'No.' I said, 'Hey, brother, ain't nobody home.'"

And Neither
Does His God

ON THE WAY OUT THE DOOR at the end of the sermon, I ask Foreman to confirm that his story was about Ali. "That's him," he says. "I know the hand of God is on him. He's being told, 'Hey, you been callin' the wrong man.' Most of his greatest gifts have been taken away, like puttin' a microscope on a fly and a pair of tweezers. Take a wing, take a leg, take this, take that, until there's nothin' left."

A Midafternoon
Dream

OLD MAN ALI IS STILL FIGHTING. Sometimes his body is classically Greek and his fists explode into radiant blurs. More often, he is not well.

I'm never actually at the fight. I'm watching TV or listening to the radio, the way I did in my father's house.

This evening, he is facing Reverend George. I'm staring down on the ring as if from heaven. At the bell for round one, Ali tosses a jab that's more a push than a punch. Foreman backs Ali to the ropes; Ali covers up. As in the first Norton fight, Ali's skin looks green under God's television lights; adipose tissue hangs in folds from his chest and hips. He's too slow to score with his punches; Foreman never connects, either. Both old warriors soon recognize the futility. They break and go to their corners, but return to the center of the ring with their stools, on which they sit and begin a debate about Islam and Christianity.

The referee is the Big Great Grand Old Hard-Ass himself, and then the ref becomes my father, who is sick and dying.

Big Old Mister White-Beard has ridden His whirlwind back to His mountaintop, leaving Ali and Foreman and my dad and me and all of us to sort this out, alone and in pain. My father is the best man I have ever known; he spent his entire life going out of his way to avoid hurting anyone. He doesn't deserve the pain and doesn't deserve to be alone.

I stand from my seat on the sofa in his house and prepare to jump into the TV screen. I've got to save my father and save Ali and save all of us.

"I'm young, I'm handsome, I'm fast, I'm pretty and can't possibly be beat," Ali said so many decades before. The irony is too obvious. Most times it's too fucking obvious. Every high school kid in love knows about irony. Wouldn't one simple unironical moment every now and then, when deserved, be more meaningful than the trillion or so ironies we could see every day, if we looked for them.

Daddy is lying on his hospital bed, shaking his head from side to side. He's carefully saved money from his small salary while raising two children by himself; he's ready to retire and enjoy himself, but here he is: he can't speak, but his head is moving from side to side and his lips are scrunched up tight and I know he doesn't want to die.

I jump straight into the TV screen. Right into the lines of blue light.

But then I wake—as usual, without getting to do anything about anything. Other than going upstairs to write about it.

I labor over this story for a couple of hours. Just when I get it down on paper and it reads as if it makes some kind of sense, I lift my head to see my own young son standing in the doorway, coming home after school and asking if I can take him out to get an ice cream.

All Things Vibrate

One

SHORTLY AFTER DAWN, a pudding-thick fog fluorescently shines, obscuring the South Carolina peat bog as the gray stretch Lincoln limousine glides up U.S. Highway 17 from Charleston airport to Myrtle Beach.

Ali is sitting directly across from me on the seat closest to the rear of the car. There are two ballpoint pens in his shirt pocket, and many streaks of blue ink mar the fabric near the pens.

"Just got back from China," he says. "When I left, five hundred thousand people followed me to the airport. A thirty-mile drive. People were there all the way . . . Been travelin' too much. I'm tired. All the stuff people make, all the things we think's important, a big wind could come up and blow it all away."

As we're talking, a documentary about Hurricane Hugo is being played on the limo's VCR. Ali has not made his "big wind" comments because of the videocassette. We pass an ancient pine forest that the driver says had been so thick before Hugo that you couldn't see twenty feet into it. The Atlantic can now be spotted a half mile to the east.

As I'm looking out the window, Ali falls asleep and begins to snore. He sits slumped with his hands in his lap. I notice for the first time how much his hairline has receded. It has been several weeks since he's had his hair colored and it has gone white at the temples. As usual, the fingers of his left hand begin to twitch. But something's different. These are not his typical tremors. As he continues to snore, the movement becomes recognizable: He's throwing short, spasmodic punches—first the jab, about once every ten seconds, and after every thirty seconds or so, he drops the straight right. Just when I begin to wonder if his health is worse than I've thought, he squints open his right eye and winks at me. When he's sure I've got his joke, he opens both eyes, sits up, and chuckles.

"Fooled you, didn't I?" he says. The old trickster is at it again, exploiting the punch-drunk rumors, the concern we all have for his health. I'm reminded of one of his favorite tactics in the latter years of his ring career—of making his legs wobble when he'd been caught with good shots, of pretending to be hurt worse than he was. But certainly, as the Ali of the 1970s was stunned when he feigned being on the verge of getting knocked into The Big Deep Canyon, the '90s version had fallen into a light sleep and had roused himself (and made me feel better) with his own joke.

✦　✦　✦　✦

ALI SAYS he got little rest on the plane from Beijing, yet two hours after he checks into a hotel, he's scheduled to make an appearance at a car dealership.

In the limo, he keeps his tinted window down so that passersby will see him. As always, when he's recognized, people wave, cheer, shout, yell. At the dealership, a crowd of hundreds is waiting. The owner of the dealership escorts Ali to a metal table and folding chair. Ali pulls one of the ballpoints from his pocket and prepares to sign.

I sit beside him and hand him tracts one by one. He signs until he gives out all he has, regularly motioning me to pass each tract to him more and more quickly, then he autographs scraps of paper, dollar bills, copies of old books and magazines, pictures of children, at least one Koran, two Bibles, and a Vietnam prisoner-of-war's photograph of himself. He leans across and whispers in my ear: "I've signed my name more than anybody in the history of the world."

This driven, crazed, marvelously insane man. Simply watching him work for hour upon hour exhausts me. So many lives! Expecting, wanting, hoping to be lifted from the dust, if only for a moment.

A roundish woman in a flowered dress appears to my left and says, "Please make it to Chuck, my husband. He's afraid to ask for himself." She turns and points. A fellow about my age but looking older, with a farmer's sun-damaged face and red, scraggly beard and swollen eyes, is leaning against the wall, hiding in the far corner. Ali tries to return the open pen to his shirt pocket and misses, staining his shirt with another blue stripe. He motions the man forward and takes his hand.

"I want you to know you're my hero," the man says, still hanging back behind his wife, embarrassed by his emotions. "You've always been my hero."

His bottom lip quivers as he speaks, and he uses the fingers of his left hand to wipe his eyes. Ali looks at him, full on, for an interminable ten seconds, wanting the fellow to know that he recognizes and honors the personal allegiance the man feels with him. Then my own eyes well up, as do Ali's, and he wipes away his tears with unsteady fingers.

✦   ✦   ✦   ✦

UPON LEAVING the dealership, Ali is scheduled to have lunch, but he wants to stop at Huntington Beach State Park, where he's been told a group of 450 inner-city children from Charlotte are being brought on buses to see the ocean for the first time in their lives. On the way, he loads up with a set of Islamic tracts from the reserve he keeps in a second, fat briefcase.

When the limo pulls into the parking lot, the kids haven't arrived. Ali steps from the car and trudges down to the beach. His ever-present dark suit and shiny shoes stand in counterpoint to the neon-bright swimwear around him.

The morning fog has burned off. It's a windless day, easily ninety degrees in the sun, and the humidity is equatorial. It's so global-warming-fry-the-planet-hot that I feel as if my flesh might melt off of my bones. Ali stands in the shade under a shelter close to the parking lot. After about fifteen minutes, the first bus rolls in. The whole hive of kids, most dressed in swim trunks, some wearing shorts, a couple with ropes tied around the waists of recently scissored-off jeans, whirl from the vehicle onto the beach, flying off in dozens of trajectories—until two of them spot Ali.

They stop, stand, and stare, pointing and elbowing each other. Ali closes his hands into fists, puts them up beside his head, and makes faces at them, sticking his upper teeth out over his lower lip. When he's certain the kids know him, he drops his arms, opens his hands, and motions them over. A few run to him. He picks up two young girls, one of them about eight years old, the other maybe ten, hugs them with uncompromising tenderness, then slowly places them back on the sand, takes their hands, and walks with them to the bus.

Soon, the other buses arrive. Teachers see Ali and race children to get to him. Kids jump up and down in front of Ali and run in circles. He performs a single magic trick nine times, making a red scarf disappear from his hand, and he signs Muslim pamphlets for children, teachers, bus drivers, and any other beachgoers who want one.

A woman in her early forties, wearing a straw hat, green plastic sandals, and a knee-length white T-shirt, runs to Ali and hugs him big and hard. He leans to kiss her on the cheek; she whispers in his ear; he turns to me. "She's goin' to Loovul," he says, arching his head to make his voice carry farther. As much as anything, I guess, that's the connection between us, at least for him—Ali's undying allegiance to his hometown, the place I met him, the city he still considers home and where I once lived.

No one seems to remember that they have come to see the ocean and to swim. Ali mock-boxes with everyone who wants to throw punches. He spots a skinny, tough-acting boy of about fourteen who's wearing knee-length cut-off jeans, a large white T-shirt, and a pair of well-worn Nikes.

Ali points, contorting his face in comically feigned anger, and squares off with the boy. The kid throws a jab toward Ali's chin and Ali slips the punch. The boy turns his back and starts to walk away, all the time cutting hard-looking eyes across his shoulder.

Ali takes a long step toward the boy, who gets scared and takes off running. Ali falls in behind. It takes him a number of steps to get going, but soon he's churning his legs so hard his knees are almost perpendicular to the ground. They race around a concrete shelter, through a field of grass and a stand of yaupon trees, then out onto the beach. Part of the time, Ali is playing fake-mean; at other moments, he's smiling and chuckling. They run probably two hundred yards down the beach at a dead sprint, this high-strung adolescent in cut-offs and the tired old giant dressed in a custom-tailored suit and shiny leather uppers, which throw small clouds of sand into the air behind him.

✦   ✦   ✦   ✦

ABOUT TWENTY of us go to dinner at an Italian restaurant. Ali and a Nation of Islam Muslim traveling with him are the only black patrons in the place. As we enter, Ali asks that I be seated across from him. After an expansive meal, he orders a piece of apple pie. Turning to me, he draws two circles in the air with his index and middle fingers. When he's certain I've understood what he wants, I ask the waitress to please add two scoops of vanilla ice cream.

Eating the pie, Ali has trouble with the fork. As he tries to cut bites, a couple of forkfuls carom off the plate and across the table-cloth. He pushes the ice cream to the side, picks up the piece of pie with his fingers, and crams it into his mouth. The Muslim seems offended. "*Ali*," he says, wincing and scowling and shaking his head, glancing at white faces around him, "do you *have* to do that?"

Ali lifts the dish and says, "I ain't nothin' but a niggah," then licks the ice cream and the remainder of the pie from the plate.

✦ ✦ ✦ ✦

BY NINE O'CLOCK, I'm fried. My eyelids are drooping, my face feels long and heavy, I can hardly speak. And, of course, I haven't just flown in from China. It's one o'clock before Ali and I reach the hotel. As I put the key in my lock, I watch him trudge away to his room and think about the grand and noble awkwardness with which he moves. Three hours later, I wake him for the drive to the airport. Ali surely wouldn't be able to go like this for more than a day or two, much less as a way of life, if he didn't regard these trips as his mission, as deeply necessary.

More than once, he's told me, "I've done so much bad, hurt so many people, I got to make up for it." Each time he has said this, I feel it rolling up from a down-deep well; he fully believes it. Yet, regardless of what he says his own motivations are (even if he is utterly certain he is doing it because he has to get clean for Allah, has to strive to remove the disease from his bloodstream through the dialysis of good works), ever since he was an adolescent he has always stepped up and outside of his own life and taken abundant, nurturing interest in people.

By six, we've checked in at the gate and he's standing in the middle of the terminal, signing tracts. He doesn't stop until five minutes after the final call for his flight. He surrounds me with his arms, then boards, the last person to get on the plane.

Two

TWO WEEKS LATER, I'm en route to Reno when the plane sucks a couple of gulls into the aft engine and we land unexpectedly at Pittsburgh International. As we wait for USAirways to find another plane, I watch a fellow on a repair crew crawl up inside the turbines, then I read a magazine, get a cup of frozen yogurt, go for a walk.

After looking around a newsstand and buying a pair of pilot's wings for Isaac, I step outside the terminal, thinking about Ali, thinking he's the only grown person I know who likes airports, even (maybe especially) the ones without retail shops. I'm reminded of the angels in one of my favorite movies, *Wings of Desire*. Like them, Ali has seen everyone, doing almost everything. None of it matters (the foibles, the scars, the pestilence); all of it resonates (the god in people).

Three crows fly over, one at a time. An elderly couple walks past, hand in hand. The man watches the crows and smiles.

A three-year-old girl with obsidian skin and huge eyes is walking across a parking lot with her mother. She's wearing a pink dress with white lace and a pair of round-toed patent-leather slippers, and her hair is pulled back neatly and is bound by a pink and white bow. "Look, Mama," the daughter says, "there's the moon."

The mother looks up. She hadn't noticed. "Yes, yes it is," she says, looking pleased.

I walk back into the terminal with a mantra for my trip. *Nothing is mundane; all things vibrate*, I silently repeat as I board the plane.

Of All Times

FROM *THE SPORT MAGAZINE BOXING HANDBOOK*, 1993

"HE COPED WITH EVERYTHING from Sonny Liston to the war in Vietnam," Hunter S. Thompson wrote of Muhammad Ali, "from the hostility of old/white draft boards to the genuine menace of Joe Frazier . . . and he has beaten every person or thing put in his way." Ali, of course, hasn't whipped every obstacle in his life. Only enough of them that we remember him as having done so.

Olympic light-heavyweight gold medalist, the only man to win the heavyweight championship of the world three times, very likely the one and only genius in the history of sport, he is not only the fastest heavyweight, he is the fastest ever fighter. Boxing historian Jim Jacobs, when studying films of Ali and middleweight Sugar Ray Robinson, found that Ali's jab was one-third faster. Witness his seldom remembered August 1966 bout with Brian London. At the beginning of round three, in two seconds' time—one Mississippi, two Mississippi—Ali knocks out London with a phantasmagoric series of *seventeen* punches. Ali's sheer ring presence rendered his opponents effectively invisible. Genius: not only was every move he made in the prize ring brilliant, but every *thought* of a move was brilliant. Grown men sitting ringside at Ali's fights were known to weep because of the beauty with which he boxed.

Outside of the ring, Ali became one of the most important people to have lived in the twentieth century and the most influential athlete ever. British filmmaker Lindsey Clennell, who is producing a ten-hour documentary about Ali's life, says more film footage has been shot of him than of anyone else in history.

We admire Ali so not only for the obvious reasons: the singular grace with which he fought for almost twenty-five years, his boastful prettiness, his huge charm and presence, his contagious and distinctive humor, his brave stand against the Vietnam War (and all war), but also for the great dignity with which he has carried himself through his stricken middle years. Indeed, a positive thing about Ali's Parkinson's disease is that it has made him seem a little less like Allah's favorite son and more like the rest of us: Ali has become everybody's favorite granddaddy: His malady has given us all the opportunity to care about him once again.

Ali today is happy and financially comfortable. Surprisingly, he occasionally boxes. I've seen him spar twice over the past five years and have been surprised on both occasions at how well he moves. One time was at a gym in Louisville, against a local heavyweight who was politely trashed by Ali for two rounds.

The second provided one of the most quietly powerful memories of my adult life.

Not long ago, there was a tribute for Ali at a community center near his farm in Berrien Springs, Michigan. At the end of the program, he loaded ten kids from a local amateur boxing club into his Winnebago and brought them home with him. Standing in his driveway at dusk, he pulled his shirttail from his trousers and slipped on a pair of old, mildewed, brown Everlast gloves. Then, under the streetlight beside his garage, Ali gave every boy a couple of rounds with him. He dropped his hands to his sides, stuck out his chin, let them bang him to the belly. He regularly punched back, sometimes purposely missing, other times careful to make only surface contact. After a couple of hours, I became sleepy. I got in my car to leave, but then just couldn't. I sat leaning over the steering wheel, where I watched The Champ and his students move around the lighted, sparkling asphalt until well past midnight.

Manila

FROM *THE SPORT MAGAZINE BOXING HANDBOOK*, 1993

THE THIRD MUHAMMAD ALI—Joe Frazier war is this great: it is impossible to sit through a viewing of the fight for the first time (or the twentieth) and not draw audible breaths of amazement.

Few of us think of Ali as a heavy puncher. Power is probably the one boxing virtue for which he hasn't received credit. In the third and final battle of the epic Frazier saga, Ali's performance informs us that the potency of his punches has been underestimated.

On the date of the fight, October 1, 1975, it would've been hard to overstate Ali's international popularity. The year before, in Kinshasa, Zaire, he had knocked out the seemingly invincible George Foreman to reclaim the world heavyweight crown that had been taken from him in April 1967 when he refused to be drafted into the United States Army. Now, Ali feels vindicated and empowered. "I am the center of the universe," he clowningly says yet seems to believe.

Although Frazier had decisioned Ali in March 1971 in one of the most dramatic fights ever fought, in January 1974 Ali had easily outpointed Smokin' Joe in a non-title bout. At thirty-one, Frazier is two years younger than Ali, but Ali believes his arch-adversary is aging badly, that he has nothing left. "It's gowna be a thrilla and a chilla and a killa when I get the gorilla in Manila," he says. He believes he'll dispose of Frazier quickly and easily; he does not train as hard as he should. Then there's the matter of Ali's personal life: unbeknownst to Belinda, his wife of seven years with whom Ali has four young children, in a secret Islamic ceremony in Zaire the week before he kayoed Foreman, Ali took a second wife, eighteen-year-old model and aspiring actress Veronica Porsche. Less than two weeks before the Frazier contest, NBC news clips from Manila feature Ali and Veronica hand in hand on their way to a presidential banquet at Malacanang Palace. President Ferdinand Marcos says to Ali, "You have a beautiful wife." Ali diplomatically replies, "No, Mister President, your wife is more beautiful." Belinda Ali sees the footage and snags the first possible flight to Manila. Confronting Ali in his hotel suite, Belinda, a black belt in karate, kicks over furniture, breaks at least one large mirror, rips down drapes, and leaves scratch marks down Ali's left cheek.

Frazier suffers from none of Ali's multi-marital concerns. Inspired by Ali's taunts (in addition to "gorilla," among a plethora of insults, Ali had called Frazier ignorant, "too ugly to be champ," and an Uncle Tom—the lowest possible indignity from one black man to another) and by a genuine dislike of his more popular foe, he prepares with almost monastic obsessiveness.

As Ali enters the ring, he looks twenty-five years old. He is whole and glowing; his level of experience is nearly transcendent; he carries himself as if he believes all fired bullets will bounce harmlessly from his torso. This will be the last night that we will see Ali's talents intact.

It is 115 degrees in the ring. From the opening bell, Ali initiates a pace that is lunatic-quick. Instead of fighting his wisest fight, dancing clockwise and counter-clockwise as he did in their second encounter, he goes straight at Frazier. He elects to stand and punch with his old foe, wanting to knock him out. In addition to beauty, there is power and danger in every Ali movement. Unexpectedly, the early rounds are predicated not on Ali's jab, but on his right. He often uses the right lead as a jab: squaring his shoulders and launching it staff-straight. This allows him to throw his most powerful punch so quickly that Frazier can't pick it off and often can't see it. Frazier's constant and underrated bobbing-and-weaving defense makes him tremendously difficult to hit, yet Ali's punches regularly catch him. Sweat flies as Frazier's head is snapped back and from side to side. Despite the punishment, Frazier's pressure is relentless; in the fourth round, as Ali begins to tire, Frazier reaches him with big shots to the abdomen, the hips, and the kidneys.

Over the next six rounds, Frazier rips Ali with huge hooks to the head and the body, as well as the occasional double right. The fighters' gloves become dramatically waterlogged by the tropical humidity, which makes these thudding blows more telling. The rounds are close and Ali wins most, but his punches are not nearly as crisp as in the first third of the fight. After the tenth, he is exhausted and, slumped on his stool, head bowed, he thinks about quitting. "I hadn't trained hard enough," he later explained to me, "but somethin' happened that never happened before or again—I took it as far as I could go, fought until I didn't have nothin' left, then God took over for me."

He goes to the well and comes up with shining buckets of life-saving water. He comes out for the eleventh and for several rounds throws the most volatile blows of a hard-punching fight. In the thirteenth, Frazier is caught with a right that turns his head through 120 degrees; his bloody mouthpiece lands in the third row of press seats. His legs quiver; he looks ready to fall. The fourteenth is more of the same: Ali's cannons roar; Frazier is repeatedly staggered and often looks on the verge of being knocked out.

Then this mad, sad, beautiful, and absurdly shattering fight ends, tenderly and perfectly. Frazier's trainer, the legendary Eddie Futch, places his hands on his supremely proud and battered fighter's shoulders. "Sit down, son," he reportedly says. "It's all over. No one will ever forget what you did here today."

Post-fight, one can't help but be deeply struck by both fighters' swollen, blanched faces and by a changed, albeit subconscious, understanding of the realities of life. "It was like death. Closest thing to dyin' I know of," Ali nakedly says to *Sports Illustrated* writer Mark Kram.

Never one to readily credit Ali, Frazier offers this: "When you see him and I," he says, "it's always gonna be a fight. That's a promise."

Ali and Frazier will never again meet one another on opposite sides of a ring with the intent of doing each other bodily harm; and neither will ever again be a complete fighter. More significantly, in this third contest both men suffered dramatic and permanent physical damage. Seventeen years to the day after it was fought, Ali watched this fight again. "Writers, experts, fans, so many people say it's my best," he said. He was sitting in his den in an overstuffed beige easy chair, marveling at his great piece of work. Throughout rounds thirteen and fourteen, while eating a bowl of vanilla ice cream, he cut his eyes around the room, pointing with his spoon and remarking to all of us who were present, "The greatest of all times," he said of himself. "Of all times."

Twenty-Dollar Bills

April 1993

THIS MORNING, I FINISHED WORK on a movie, my first, and it was the single worst writing experience I've had. I need to cleanse myself, get away from Hollywood types, reconnect with something that, and someone who, feels good and right and real. Leaving the producer's penthouse office in Century City, I hop a taxi to a South Central shop called Book Soup, where Ali is signing customer copies of Howard's newly published volume of Ali photographs.

Hundreds are waiting. Ali and Howard are scheduled for two hours but sign for better than three, until a half hour after the shop has closed. I stand behind Ali's chair and watch. Although I've seen similar scenes dozens of times, I never tire of witnessing the ways (and the moments) that people connect with The Champ. As I leave the shop with Ali and Howard, in the darkened alley near where Howard's car is parked, a blond, light-skinned man wearing navy-colored clothing and standing back and away in the shadows urges a maybe ten-year-old blond boy to approach Ali. The boy is carrying a pair of old, scuffed cordovan boxing gloves that he hesitantly lifts over his own head. "Will you sign 'Cassius Clay 1960'?" the boy asks.

Ali, Howard, the shadowed opportunist, his embarrassed son, and I: each of us understands that these mitts will be sold as an authentic pair of Cassius Clay's Olympic championship gloves. Does Ali mind? He takes a pen from the boy's hand and unhesitatingly signs exactly as asked.

"How long you in L.A.?" he asks as we turn and head for the car.

"I'm on my way home," I say. "Haven't seen my wife and kids in almost a month." And: "Do you think Howard'd give me a ride to LAX?"

Ali waves me into the backseat while Howard eases in behind the wheel. As we pull out of the parking lot, Ali asks, "What you workin' on?" without turning to look at me in the backseat.

"I just finished a movie," I say. "Hated doing it. The whole thing was so bad I couldn't sleep at night. And I couldn't eat. I lost over ten pounds."

Ali looks puzzled. "Why?" he asks, interested.

"Hated working with the producer. I wanted to quit every day. I stayed with it for one reason—to pay the mortgage.

"What I want to write about is my friendship with you," I continue, sure that this will make him happy. "I feel I'm saying something true and real and cleansing every time I do."

Ali hesitates only a moment before replying. "Millions of people want to be friends with me. I can't even remember your name," he says, surprising me not with that fact but with his hardness of tone. "You shoulda written about me when I wanted to be written about."

"I was a kid," I say. "I was in junior high and high school."

To our right, a group of middle-aged men and one heavy old woman wearing a loose purple and gray skirt and a black chef's hat are standing at a bus stop under a streetlight, the sky salmon-colored with city lights and the recently set sun. Ali raises a trembling left finger and points, motioning Howard to pull over. As we come to a stop, I count nine men, several of them Ali's age and older.

Ali rolls out of the car and approaches the biggest one, a block-bod-ied, tough-acting fellow who has a shaved giant's pate and is wear-ing a white T-shirt with arms bigger around than my trouser legs. "Give me Joe Frazuh, I want Joe Frazuh," Ali shouts, unbuttoning his jacket. "You look like Joe Frazuh," he exclaims, pointing the index finger of his jab hand, half-prancing toward the big man, pumping playful punches in the air.

When he's maybe five feet away from the Joe Frazier doppelganger, Ali breaks off and whirls toward a different stunned, laughing man and then another and another, slinging light playful shots at each of them, after which he chucklingly slaps hands with several men and leans to kiss the grizzled and nearly toothless old woman on her grinning cheek, almost knocking her chef's hat to the ground, her eyes now richly alive when not a moment before they were showing an entire adult life of resignation. "Champ, when we were growing up, you meant everything to us," someone behind me says.

A slightly/delicately closed-mouth-smiling, satisfactorily satiated Ali heads for the car and I expect that we'll be leaving. Instead, he stops, reaches into his jacket pocket, and produces his wallet while turning and stepping back toward the bus stop. As is often the case with Ali, people have arrived as if talismanically summoned, and there are now maybe forty of us on this corner, many irradiated by the streetlight, a few deep in shadow. As Ali's right hand trembles, he opens the wallet and works to control his fingers as he tugs out twenty-, fifty-, and one-hundred-dollar bills, which he hands one at a time to every person present. He gives away all the money he has with him, thousands of dollars that I suppose he was paid by the book shop.

"Stay here," he says to the still-growing crowd when he has emp-tied his wallet. "I'll be back."

He takes a seat next to me in the rear of the car. As we pull away from the curb, he leans forward and almost silently says "ATM" to

Howard, then falls back hard, closes his eyes, rubs his face, and begins to lightly snore. At the first bank we come to, under green and orange lights at the ATM, Ali fills his wallet with new twenties.

It takes us maybe thirty minutes to make the round trip. When we arrive back at the bus stop, except for the otherworldly, pale-orange, gauzy lights of the city, the sky is dark. Roughly twenty-five people have waited for Ali. He's tired now. Without playing, he gives out crisp new bills to everyone. A strong-smelling, ash-gray old guy who looks a little like Ali's dead father places a broad thumb over his tracheotomy hole and, with an electronic alien rasping noise—a sound from the tremulous far side of the River Styx—he asks Ali to sign his twenty. Ali autographs the bill and then hands him a replacement. "No wine," he says. "No cigarettes. This is for food."

Howard drives to the airport while Ali sleeps beside me. As we slow and stop in front of the USAirways terminal, Ali blinks himself awake. "Glad you were here," he says as I open my door. "Enjoyed seein' you."

And, as I step away from Howard's vehicle: "Davy," he says, pointing straight at my face—or, more precisely, the knockout area of my jaw—his eyes alight, not quite winking at me. "Now don't you write none of this."

Eleven Ghosts

One
AUGUST 1993

THE PLACE LOOKS SO UNINTERESTING, so forgotten and unimportant, that I drive past without recognizing where I am; we have to turn around and go back.

I park across the road beside the small white mosque and the block-shaped, one-room, knotted-cedar cabins in which sparring partners and other entourage members slept. We get out of the rented van, Lyn, Johanna, Isaac, and I. We've been on holiday in the mountains of West Virginia and western Pennsylvania for a week. Before we left home, I called Ali at a Beverly Hills hotel to ask if it would be okay to visit the Deer Lake training camp.

"My man," he said as he answered the phone. "Where you been? Haven't seen you in a while."

There was the unmistakable sound of the receiver being dropped. After waiting without success for him to pick it up, I hung up the line.

I tried to call back a few times over the next ten minutes; each time, there was a busy signal. When I finally got through, he picked up on the second ring. "Dropped the phone," he said by way of greeting. His statement was not an apology, and, as always, there was no trace of embarrassment. As many calls as he gets, I don't know how he knew that the person on the other end of the line would be me. Or if he did know.

Now, while the kids climb on the boulders and play with an orange cat, I walk around the cabins, dutifully trying to feel something. Everything is much smaller than I remember, like visiting your elementary school as an adult. The buckboard is almost exactly where I'd last seen it, behind the building that once housed the ring. Much of the paint on many of the rocks, expertly applied by Cash, has been faded by sun and wind and washed away by rain and snow.

There's one fixture I haven't seen—a large granite tombstone that reads ALI'S STAFF, placed to the right of the entrance to the gym by Bundini when camp broke before the Larry Holmes fight in 1980. Seventeen names are inscribed on the monument, including Bingham's, Bundini's, and Angelo Dundee's; Jimmy Ellis is also there, as well as others I'll never meet, some of whom have tombstones in other places.

We take photos of the kids sitting on the rocks and of Isaac giving me a high-five while standing on Sonny Liston. Lyn climbs atop old Jack Johnson; I snap a shot. She and I step across the road and stand beside the van, looking down on the gym and on the Ali living quarters and the kitchen. "Stay here," I say after a minute or two.

I walk back down the hill, still trying to feel something, looking for some sign of the owner, thinking it might work better if I trudge around by myself. I peek in windows at empty walls and bare floors rich with dust, turn rusted doorknobs, steal a long-arm-sized piece of bark from the side of the cabin where I had once sparred Ali. I figure I'll frame it with a picture of the two of us together and hang it on the wall behind my desk. As I pull the crumbling wood from the wall, a droplet of water splashes the back of my hand. I look behind me; a long black cloud is moving in from across the west side of the mountain. A second, tumescent drop hits me square in the eye.

I jog up the hill to the van, passing the kids as I cross the road. By the time I get the doors unlocked, the air is fragrant with rain; quarter-size drops drub a syncopated rhythm on the hood. We scramble in and start the engine, barely beating a first-class downpour.

A few miles down the road, headed for Amish country with the windshield wipers on high, I find a public radio station and catch the last few wild bars of a Celtic war song. "That was James Galway and the Chieftains performing 'The Red Admiral Butterfly,'" a woman announcer says in a husky Scottish brogue, a voice of mist and meadow, forest and dreams.

"Our next and final song," she says, "was written by blind harper Turlough O'Carolan. O'Carolan, known as the last great itinerant Irish harper, died on the twenty-fifth of March, 1738, at the age of sixty-eight. He had traveled to Aldeford, to the home of his lifetime patron and sponsor. When he arrived at the house, he called for his harp and wrote and played 'Carolan's Farewell to Music.' He then retired to bed, where he died."

As the centuries-old melody wafts from the speakers, I ask Lyn what she thinks of the old Ali haunt. "It was all right," she says, "but I didn't feel any of his greatness there."

She sounds surprised and disappointed. I tell her it makes sense that she wouldn't. It confirms what one-eighth-Irish-mystic Ali has said just about every time I've been with him. "All the things I've done, all the praise, all the fame, don't none of it mean nothin'. It's all only dust."

Two

IT HAS TURNED COLD in Michigan, which surprises me. When I get to the farm, I'm wearing khaki shorts and a T-shirt that features a photo of Ali spanking Floyd Patterson in their first bout.

As I step from the car, the new groundskeeper, a bespectacled fellow who reminds me of an old New England sea captain, sees raised hairs on my legs and goes over to the gym, returning with a pair of blue warm-ups I've often seen Ali wearing. "Here, put these on," he says, handing me the pants.

Floyd's no longer at the farm. Although I wonder where he's gone, there's no use asking Ali. People come into, and go from, Ali's life all the time.

Men's Journal has sent a photographer with me, a guy I like a lot, who has a gentle demeanor and a kind of mystery about him, as well as a plenty wonderful name—Len Irish. Len asks me to take off my shirt and stand at the fence beside the barn. He takes a shot of me wearing Ali's britches pulled all the way up to my shoulders.

✦   ✦   ✦   ✦

INSIDE, I INTRODUCE Len to Lonnie, then to Ali, who's at his desk. Ali stands when he sees us. Len visibly trembles as he reaches for Ali's hand.

"Davy," Ali says, "my man." Ali asks what I'm working on, other than my new story about him. I tell him I'd like to ride on the space shuttle and write a book about the experience. "I'll be The Greatest Writing Astronaut of All Times," I say in my best Ali voice, which has improved from spending so much time with The Man himself. And I'm interested in hanging out with and writing about Jimmy Carter, I tell him.

"He's smart," says Ali. "Buildin' houses for poor people. Doin' it with his own hands. I got all the money I need. Want to give every penny I make from now on to charities, to help people. Don't matter if I make forty-three million. Gonna give it all away." I'm sure that, in this moment, Ali almost believes what he has just said.

Len excuses himself to go outside and set up for our portrait. I stay behind, telling Ali about my writing and how much I like what I'm doing. "When I was young, I always knew there'd be somebody like you," he says. "Always knew you'd come along."

"You mean that, don't you?" I say. "You did know, didn't you?"

He nods.

"How did you know?" I ask.

He can't say.

But maybe I can. Or at least I can propose a theory. Ali's proclamation isn't founded simply in the freedom of an illusion that is borne out by facts. Nor is it so much arrogance as it is a sure sense of his own destiny. Perhaps he was born to live out a mythology, to reveal for us, among other things, the dharma of self-importance. And maybe I'm one of the vehicles that relays this myth. Or maybe the mythology is only my own. Either way, one of its morals is that we cannot invent ourselves, that the modern religion of self-actualization is a current cultural delusion.

"I didn't make myself and you didn't make yourself," Ali has often told me. "All the things people praise me for, I didn't do those myself. We don't choose to draw air into our own lungs. We don't decide where we're born or who we are."

✦ ✦ ✦ ✦

ON THIS VISIT, as on every other before or since, the one predictable thing about Ali is that the *I am* of him sloshes out of the pails we attempt to carry him in. As Len sets up his first shot, at a place near the pool where he likes the quality of light and the view of trees near the horizon, Ali opens a storage room, and pulls out flotation rings and a half-inflated plastic float, which he plops into the deepest water. Right beside the float is a young beautiful rabbit, on its side, dead, among yellow and brown leaves. Ali seems not to see the rabbit. Watching me, Ali, who can't swim a lick, convincingly pretends he's going to walk off the edge and into nine feet of water.

Ali's facial features have recently taken on yet more of the muscular rigor of Parkinsonism. Despite this, when Len is ready, Ali allows him to take shot after tight shot of his face on roll after roll of film.

By early afternoon, the day has warmed considerably. Weathercasters are warning of a late-summer stormfront that's stampeding across the plains and Lake Michigan. The front will be accompanied by dramatic hail, sustained seventy-five-mile-per-hour winds, and possibly tornadoes. Though the sun is out, it's already begun to lightly rain. As Len shoots photos, I stand to Ali's right, brushing raindrops from his hair. An hour later, as we ready ourselves to go back in the house, knowing that Len can't possibly get an informal photo with the kind of equipment he's brought and the way he has it set up, Ali opens the door to the garage and rides out on a neon-yellow bicycle, which he tools once around the driveway as Len rolls

his eyes over the missed shot. Ali then puts the bike away and asks
if I'd like to go for a ride in the Rolls, which he proceeds to drive
bouncingly through the fields as if it were a plow.

As we step from the car with me still wearing Ali's pants and
the T-shirt with his image on the back, Len has finally removed his
camera from its tripod and has attached a lens he can use for candid
action. As Len shoots away, Ali squares off with me and we toss a
few punches at one another. "I could be your son," I say, "if I was
black."

Inside the house, as Ali and I wait for Len to set up a second
portrait near the pond, Ali listens to a Little Richard cassette with a
tinny, vibrating jam box pressed up against his right cheek, though
he's standing less than ten feet away from a three-thousand-dollar
stereo system. As "Tutti-Frutti" is being drilled into his inner ear,
with his eyes closed, Ali points at the speaker, shouting, "The King,
the King," speaking of the singer and not of himself.

Len comes in to say he's ready. Ali motions for him to sit at the
kitchen table, where Ali proceeds to serve us vanilla ice cream hon-
orifically, with high sacrament, studying Len's face and mine to see
if we properly appreciate his gift, which is not so much the ice cream
as it is his act of giving. Of the thirty or so meals I've taken with Ali
and/or have seen him eat, vanilla ice cream has been served with
probably twenty of them.

Outside, Ali takes a seat on a stool Len has set up on high ground
above the pond. Parkinson's has made Ali's eyes inordinately sensi-
tive to light; for this reason, he typically wears sunglasses in public.
Now, with wind and light rain and sun making direct contact with
his face, he blinks rapidly, almost uncontrollably. "Don't need this
shit no more," he says to me of the photo session. "Doin' this as a
favor for you."

Other than Howard's photos, this has been the first group of por-
traits I know of that Ali has sat for in years. I tell Len that we've got

enough, we have all the pictures we need. "Man, this makes me feel bad," I tell The Champ. "I'm sorry I asked you to do this."

He turns his head, studying me, gets up from the stool, and with me beside him, starts back toward the house. He drops his long arm across my shoulders and (at my expense) tells me the single worst joke I have ever heard. "A chicken ain't nothin' but a bird," he says. "A white man ain't nothin' but a turd. And a niggah . . . ain't nothin'."

✦   ✦   ✦   ✦

LEN AND I take Ali and Lonnie to dinner in St. Joseph. As we wait for our meal and Ali signs autographs for waiters and kitchen staff and customers, I mention to Lonnie that Ali seems pleased with the big-screen TV a local merchant recently gave him. "When he's home," she says, "he watches news hour after hour. The only thing that makes him turn it off is when he wants to play with his new pet."

"I didn't think he cared anything about dogs and cats," I say.

"This is a big animal. Didn't you see it out in the pasture? Why don't you mention it in your story? This fan in Africa gave him a rhinoceros."

"Gave him a what?"

"A rhinoceros. As big a fan as you are, Davy, you must've heard about Muhammad's rhino."

"No, no, tell me about it," I say.

She laughs out loud and turns away, blushing. "April Fool's," says the wife of The Number One Jokester of All Times.

✦   ✦   ✦   ✦

WHEN THE BILL COMES, I pull my MasterCard from my wallet. The waitress takes it, but soon returns and leans close to my ear. "Your card was declined, sir," she says softly.

Damn *Sport* magazine. All those thousands of dollars in travel expenses my editor has required me to put on my card, and that he hasn't repaid. This *would* be the time that I exceed my limit.

Without my asking, Lonnie quickly snaps a card down on the waitress's tray. Embarrassed, instead of looking at Lonnie, I stare at the floor, then up at the tray. The American Express card Lonnie has placed on the tray reads G.O.A.T. (Greatest of All Times), INC.

"I ain't nothin' but an old goat," Ali snickers from across the table.

Three

AS LEN IRISH DEVELOPS PHOTOS to be run with the article I've written, he phones me. "Picture after picture," he says, "he looked awful in every one, looked like he's wearing a mask of Ali's face. Just when I thought nothing good would come out, there it was—this one photo. He looks like the Mona Lisa. Timeless, satisfied, spiritual.

"You know, Ali was in town last week," Len continues. "This is going to sound silly, but I kept expecting him to give me a call. I spent those few hours with him and he makes you feel so close to him, you think he's your friend.

"I was kind of disappointed he didn't call," Len concludes, chuckling.

Len Irish's portrait of Ali

Four

MRS. ODESSA GRADY CLAY dies in August 1994. She was the same age her husband had been at his death, seventy-seven. Her death hits Ali deep and hard.

In November, Lonnie invites me to the first fundraising dinner for the Muhammad Ali Center, a museum to be dedicated to Ali, his legacy, and what's left of his memorabilia. Johanna, Isaac, and I drive to Louisville for the dinner and, more essentially, to hang out with Ali, Lonnie, and Asaad. Isaac and I watch the Michael Moorer–George Foreman world heavyweight championship bout with Ali and Asaad in their suite at the old and storied Brown Hotel.

Actually, that's not entirely true. Only two of us watch the fight. Two of us chase each other around the room. Moorer–Foreman is the only boxing match I've seen in a year. I've stopped writing about people who punch one another in the head and body. This past summer, I managed to sell a couple of pieces of short fiction. More recently, I've chosen not to be working, hoping to rest and heal up. Lyn and I are going through a second, and final, divorce. I understand much of what she finds frustrating about our lives together. She sees me on TV or hears me on the radio—"acting like hot shit," she says, believing the last word of that phrase is true of me, if not the first or third—all the time getting more and more burned-up that I can't pay the bills like people who work in a viable profession.

From my point of reference, at forty-two, I've finally evolved out of my romance for physical jabbing (boxing, martial art) and feel that it's time to grow out of a relationship where emotional jabbing has long been regarded as acceptable behavior. So. Here I am with grand-pappy Ali again, hoping my life will fall back into shape. I've not seen Ali for a long while, mostly because I don't have the money to travel, and magazine and newspaper editors no longer pay my expenses to hang out with him.

All during this visit, he looks removed, as if from another dimension, as if he's staring at the world from the other side of a glass. Earlier today, as he moved from appearance to appearance (first at a Catholic high school, then at a cousin's Caribbean restaurant, later stopping a circus parade dead in the street, horses and elephants and people and all: a highwire artist ran up, shouting, "Muhammad Ali, Muhammad Ali. I live for you, man," tugging on my arm, begging me to take his photo with The Champ), there were often globules of drool on his bottom lip. When he noticed them, he sucked on his lip, bent his head, tugged at the left lapel of his suit jacket, and discreetly caught spittle near the inside breast pocket. A label had been sewn into Ali's jacket lining. THE GREATEST, it read in red Arabic-style stitchery.

Three-year-old Asaad remains large for his age. He's heavier than nine-year-old Isaac; the two boys are nearly the same height. Ali is lying on the bed; I'm sitting in a chair beside him. As Ali and I try to watch the fight (and I'm watching Ali watch the fight), the boys stop running in front of the TV screen when—and only when—Ali's name is spoken by announcers. Asaad freezes where he stands, turns to the television, then to his father, and proclaims, "They said 'Muhammad Ali,' Daddy." He and Isaac then resume the chase.

In the ring, Foreman is wearing the faded and shabby red-and-blue trunks he'd worn in his knockout loss to Ali twenty years before. Trailing on every judge's scorecard, in the eleventh round Foreman kayos Moorer with a magically timed overhand right to the jaw. At forty-six, Reverend George has become the oldest-ever world heavyweight champion.

"I'm glad for him, glad for him," Ali says without hesitation when I ask what he feels. I notice that he's wearing a new timepiece. He likely broke the last one mock-boxing with someone somewhere (everyone everywhere). I've never known him to wear a digital. Every watch he's worn has had a classic clear round face. Always a clear face that protects those sweeping hands, which remind him that we are on a rotating dust mote that is speeding through the vast, vast cosmos.

At the end of the Moorer–Foreman telecast, Ali wires a congratulatory telegram to Foreman in Las Vegas.

After breakfast the next morning, I hug Ali goodbye, not knowing that this will be the last time I'll see him for twenty years.

*Ali and Isaac Miller (Asaad Ali and Johanna Miller
in background), Louisville, November 1994*

Interlude: Marrakech

MID-JUNE 1996

NINE A.M. *The Champ answers his phone. "Ali," I say, happy to hear his voice. "How are you?"*

"Got somethin' hap'nin'," he says, easy to understand. Before eleven, he's usually sharper, has more energy, and speaks more distinctly. "My man. I cain't talk now. Trainin' for somethin', gotta go. Call me later."

Over the next weeks, I call Berrien Springs seven, maybe eight times. Each time, the office phone doesn't ring, but clicks over to voicemail. The house phone is always busy, too, and so is the fax machine. In the years I've known him, this has never happened.

In early July, the editor of Sport asks me to spend three weeks in Rabat, Marrakech, Casablanca, and Fez with King Hassan II of Morocco, and write a travel piece centered on the king's ultraritzy pro-am golf tournament. (King Hassan is obsessed with golf; one of the most massive of his twenty-plus palaces is rumored to house an eighteen-hole PGA-level course.) I haven't written a magazine story in three years, and my first book is scheduled for publication next month; I'm nervous about it and don't want to leave home. But although I know zilch about golf and have less than zero interest in King Hassan II and, at most, minor curiosity about Morocco, as a favor to my longtime editor, I accept the assignment.

In Marrakech on the morning of July 20, I ride the hotel elevator down to the first floor for breakfast. After I eat, I'm going to leave for a day trip high up into the Atlas Mountains, far away from clownishly dressed, rich American golfers and the glaringly ostentatious king of a poor country.

As I round the corner after stepping from the elevator, I see a group of eight or nine people—Americans, Europeans, and Moroccans—clustered at the concierge's desk. Everybody's eyes are fixed on one spot; no one is moving and several men are wiping away tears. I walk to the left of the group and toward the restaurant. As I pass, I glance over and see who everyone is watching on a small television. There's a shock in seeing him, standing alone under the lights, the world behind him darkened, his skin the same hue as the polished Lebanon cedar of the concierge's desk. And then I smile. This is what he's been training for. Ali. Ahh-lee! Thirty, maybe thirty-five pounds lighter than when I last saw him. Standing near the top of the Atlanta Olympic stadium, dressed all in white, raising a dramatically shaking right arm over his head while holding a lighted torch.

✦ ✦ ✦ ✦

I ASK THE CONCIERGE to cancel my day trip. Leaving the hotel, I walk for miles with no plan for where I might land. Almost everything around me has stopped. Nearly everywhere I look, small groups of people are standing still and watching replays of Ali's illuminated image through the windows of shops and restaurants. Very few cars and motorbikes are on the normally busy streets, even fewer carts and donkeys. Marrakech has stopped. The air around me sounds and feels quiet and still and weighted. Quiet as a rural North Carolina February morning following an unexpected four-inch snowfall.

Hardly noticing where I am or what I'm doing, I enter Souk Semmarine and almost immediately get startled out of my Ali reverie by a loudly chanting group of men as they run past me, carrying a plainly wrapped, incensed corpse on a canvas-covered wood board resting on top of their shoulders. I wind through booths filled with iridescent kaftans and pashminas, into Souk el Attarine and its gleaming copper and brass lanterns, tarnished silver teapots and cups, dusty oil lamps and dangling earrings and a riot of smell from dozens of spice booths. All around me, in nearly every booth, men of all ages stand holding tiny battery-operated TVs, openly weeping as Moroccan television plays and replays and then once more plays the image of Ali shakingly lighting the flame half a world away. "Baraka frassek," a lamb- and camel-leather merchant says to his little Sony TV as I pass. "Baraka frassek"—blessings be on your head.

✦   ✦   ✦   ✦

NOT ONLY MARRAKECH. The planet stops. To hundreds of millions of people the world round, Ali instantaneously becomes who I've understood him to be since 1988: superman, who has become everyman and thereby another form of superman. He is family. He is us. We are him.

Act Three

A Hymn for Agnostics

There Is Nothing
in the Universe
That You Are Not

September 23, 2014

LATE AFTERNOON, THE FIRST DAY OF FALL. Horizon to horizon deep-shadowed light. Light that reveals, that makes everything seem more real than other days, than yesterday—and, strangely, more of a dream, less real.

It's been twenty years since I last saw him. Twenty-five since I've lived in Kentucky. Twenty-six since I met him and my world was transformed. People at the Muhammad Ali Center have asked me to speak about The Champ and my friendship with him during the week leading up to the Center's annual Ali Humanitarian Awards. Although Ali rarely travels, if his health allows, he'll be there.

For years now, like Ali, I've seldom left home. While on assignment in Asia more than a decade ago, I was kidnapped and held captive for three weeks. Ever since, regardless of money and circumstances, I no longer hire myself out to magazines, preferring to toil on my own books. With no monthly (or sometimes even yearly) stipend, I'm usually broke, but mostly content. My days are spent writing, walking in the woods with my wife Kat and our dogs, and watching after our two-year-old son Sam.

Waiting for the elevator in Louisville's Galt Hotel, I'm gazing out of a fourteenth-floor full-wide picture window, staring down onto the I-64 artery, half-clogged with the plaque of evening traffic. Red lights of an ambulance move quickly in an easterly direction; in a westerly lane, blue police lights sit immobile behind an abandoned dark car.

The Ali Center stands a fifth of a mile away, neon tubes on its multi-colored ceramic-tile facade glowing softly, reservedly, respectably near the top of the six-story, angular, modernist wall: Green: MUHAMMAD. Red: ALI. White: CENTER.

To the right, the half-mile-wide Ohio chugs slowly and determinedly south under that fabled bridge, the one from which Cassius Marcellus Clay Jr. is reputed to have thrown his 1960 Olympic gold medal. "Never did that," Ali told me more than a quarter of a century ago, shortly after we'd first met. "That story was Herbert's. Came up with it for a book. Tryin' to make me into some kind of George Washington for black folks. Never threw my medal off no bridge. Just lost it, that's all."

Stepping into the lobby of the Center, the first person I see, standing directly in front of me: Mrs. Yolanda Ali, who's listening to a short, thin, moneyed-looking woman in her early seventies who's wearing a pink- and orange-flowered silk dress. Lonnie looks up, sees me over the top of the woman's head, blinks, and releases a sigh of surprise. "Excuse me," she says, touching the woman's sleeve and nodding toward me, "this is a man I haven't seen in . . ."

"Twenty years," I say from the other side of the room.

"Twenty years," she repeats, stepping across the thirty feet and the three decades between us. As we reach each other she hugs me long and tight. "Davy," she says. "We wondered what happened to you. Muhammad thought you might be dead."

"Not yet," I say, chuckling. "But I did get kidnapped in Hong Kong.

After I escaped, I started getting serious threats against my kids and me. I had to disappear."

She nods. "You've been living off the grid," she says, knowingly.

I nod in return. "Way off. No phone, no Internet, no credit cards, no bank accounts, no bills in my name. But I can't take it anymore. It's time to stick my face up out of the foxhole. I'm remarried and my wife and I have a new son. . . . Things are going pretty good. . . . How are you, Lonnie?"

"Good," she says. And, after a moment, "Getting old." She turns and looks over her shoulder as if someone in a secret recess might smite her for this confession. Then: "New son?" she exclaims. "Davy, you're going to be ninety years old before he starts college."

"I know, I know," I say, abashed by my own foolhardiness. "And I thought Muhammad and you were crazy to have Asaad as late as you did."

Other than wrinkles around and under her eyes and the fact that her face is a little thinner and cheekbones more prominent, Lonnie looks basically the way she did in the mid-1990s. "You look terrific," I say and mean it, recognizing how very difficult it must be to care for Muhammad in his advanced stage of Parkinson's. It stuns me how well she's wearing her burden, refusing, like Ali himself, to bow to the weight of the world. Indeed, as she and I talk over the next fifteen minutes, I recognize that, over the years, this very strong woman has been made wise by her love for, and life with, Muhammad. In Japan, people speak of *musho no ai*, which translates roughly as "love that expects no compensation." To the Japanese people, *musho no ai* is the highest possible love. It's understatement to say that the wife and caregiver of our planet's first fully international personality has mansions of selfless love for her husband. "Come with me," she now says, taking me by the hand. "Muhammad will want to see you."

I follow her up wide bright stairs, turning right around a dark corner, going right again through an open door and onto a short thin dark hallway. Time suddenly goes strange: it speeds up, slows down, ceases to exist. Perception ripples and snaps like a flag in a stiff wind. *This is inevitable, all of this is inevitable, has always been inevitable*, I hear and feel myself think. Another turn, another shorter hallway. Compress, compress. An open doorway, a room ahead of us, brightening. Opening, opening . . . Twenty years, twenty years . . .

Here it comes. This is the moment. Compress, compress . . .

Release.

There he is, at the far end of the room, framed against refracted light from the pale bright wall. As always, as soon as I see him, everyone and everything else recedes. I have no idea if Lonnie has stepped through the open doorway with me.

There he is, perfectly framed and alone on all four sides as if he were an exhibit in a gallery, a lost Edward Hopper. There, sunk deep back in a gray wheelchair, motionless as a photograph on a magazine page waiting to be turned.

Not a sports magazine, not a news magazine. This time it's *National Geographic*. A special issue about an Egyptian exhibition at the Smithsonian's Museum of Man. This photo is of the newly discovered, copper-sheened, unprecedentedly preserved mummy of Ramses the Great. Or of Ali the Greatest, unveiled here and now, in this moment, in this exact moment, for the very first time. Dressed not in pharaoh garb, but in blue-collar rural American: small-checked blue-and-white button-up shirt; worn-looking blue-black jeans that would have been the correct size for the 220-pound man who long ago dominated the entirety of sport (and of my consciousness); cinched-up-extra-tight tan-colored belt that ensures his pants won't fall down; huge almost brick-square black shoes and tight black over-the-calf stretch socks that unintentionally serve to accentuate the size of his shrunken legs (those formerly extraordinary limbs that, half a century before, lifted him and kept him from harm as surely and beautifully as if he were winged), each of which has now been whittled down to a circumference no greater than that of a Midwest kitchen-table farm chair.

Walking toward him, I have to push away the thought that this isn't Ali, that this cannot possibly be the prismatic person, the incomparably expansive man, the singular cosmic force that I have known. Then I have to push away that thought a second time, thinking, *Ali's no less than he's always been. He's safe in this shell.* As I approach, he closes his eyes. As I kneel beside him, he opens them.

"Do you remember me, Champ? It's been a long time. You saved my life. If it weren't for you, I would've been dead in a ditch long ago."

Without turning his head, Ali looks at me out of the left corners of his eyes. Looks at me thoroughly. He opens them wider, acknowledging me, letting me know that he does remember, or maybe is pretending to.

"It's been a long time. We used to hang out in the '80s and '90s. I became a writer because of you. I used to write about you for magazines and newspapers. You've given me a very rich life. I'm sorry I don't look like I used to. I've changed a lot." Every word is said in the rushed, crowded, tearful, and portentous manner of the things I wish I'd said to my father before he died. "I'm getting old," I say, echoing Lonnie's evaluation of herself.

Without moving one-tenth of an inch, Ali's facial features seem to gravitate toward mine. Slowly reaching for my left hand, he takes it in his, looks at me a weighted moment, and closes his eyes. His touch is cooler than the air in this room and even gentler than it had been when I last saw him; it's no heavier than that of my twenty-five-pound two-year-old when I'm carrying him against my chest and he touches me on the bare back of my neck with particularly tender intention. Ali's massive hand and fingers surround, envelop, then cocoon mine. Because of his dramatic weight loss, the boxing-induced calcium deposits on the knuckles of his second and fourth fingers look mountainous and craggy. I stare at our hands together and close my eyes, tilting my head slightly back and up to some place above the walls and outside this room. *Is anybody watching? Is anyone listening?* I wonder. For the next few minutes, neither of us opens his eyes.

Tonight's Dream

One

FOLLOWING MY PRESENTATION at the Center, back in my room at the Galt, a little shocked and more than a little sad, troubled, and diminished by the Ali I've just witnessed, I think about calling Kat, hoping that hearing her voice and talking with her will make me feel better. As I click on the lamp over the small reading desk and pull the phone from my pocket, music from the floor above or maybe the room to the left starts thumping the air and making the walls and windows tremble.

I step over to the picture window at the far end of the room, wanting to know where the cranium-busting bass is coming from. After I talk with Kat, I'd like to order room service, eat a light meal, read a few pages, and sit with my feelings about Ali. And maybe try to write some. But there'll be no way to get any of that done with this music pounding the floors, the walls, my head, emotions, and thoughts.

I open the curtains to the outside. Night has suddenly dropped in like something too heavy to hold; the moon is high, pale, thin, and lacking in heft. In the middle distance, the Ali Center is large and illuminated by spotlights, looking like a fancy cruise ship sailing atop an impenetrably dark sea. On the sports-stadium-sized court-

yard directly below my window, I'm surprised to find the source of
the music—an East Indian cultural festival with food booths, an
elevated stage and musicians, including a guy on a booming syn-
thesizer; another thrumming an electric bass guitar; a very active
tabla player; and three more men, each of whom is playing a variety
of percussion instruments that I don't recognize. Dozens of women,
children, and a few men have congregated in front of the stage,
where they're whirling and spinning in one large circle as if around
centuries of open fires, every man on this wheel wearing browns
and grays, each woman and female child brightly dressed in flowing, shimmering saris of melding orange, yellow, green, purple, and
blue. I consider leaving the hotel and walking over to the festival to
buy a plate of *aloo palak* and a couple of big pieces of *naan*, and to
closely watch the dancers, but then think better of it. I very much
want to be alone, and I'm getting precisely what I need: this shel-
tered, privileged view from above. In my small, dimly lighted room
I'm afforded tonight's fully necessary dream of transcendence.

Two

SEPTEMBER 29, 2014

*(the thirty-seventh anniversary of the date Lyn and I hoped
to get married at the Ali–Earnie Shavers fight)*

ALI AND I ARE SITTING in the Center's library, a handsome,
bird's-eye-maple-trimmed, elevated room that's enclosed on two sides
by wide, tall windows that overlook the Center's main lobby. The
Ali library is a small, brightly lighted, friendly-feeling, and studious-
looking space that houses his United States Presidential Medal of
Freedom and hundreds of the innumerable books and films about
him. Around the corner from the library, his British Broadcasting
Corporation and *Sports Illustrated* Athlete of the Century awards are
displayed in glass cases. All of these awards were received late in life,
when Lonnie could keep Ali from giving them away. On two separate
occasions when I was visiting with him in the early '90s in Berrien
Springs, he tried to give me significant-looking trophies, plaques, and
awards. I sometimes wish I'd accepted them, knowing that if I'd done
so, they would've eventually found a home here in the Center.

Ali has not said word one to me over the several days I've been
with him. People at the Center have told me that they haven't heard
him speak in more than three years. This afternoon, he's sunk deep

down in his wheelchair, I'm sitting to his left on a leather-cushioned maple desk chair, leaning toward him. He's dramatically stooped at the shoulders, head down and folded over his lap; his eyes are closed and have been much of this afternoon.

A skinny, freckled, red-haired kid in his early twenties, wearing jeans and a gray long-sleeved T-shirt, who's carrying a pair of cheap red-vinyl Everlast gloves he assuredly wants autographed, creaks open the door we'd forgotten to lock. He sees Ali, widens his eyes, and steps slowly into the room, softly closing and locking the door behind him.

Unreservedly staring at Ali, he lowers the gloves to his right side and, within moments, drops them to the floor, leaving them as he quickly strides toward us, almost running. "Champ, Champ," the kid says, now standing three feet from Ali, fiercely, dramatically, almost uncontrollably weeping. "Look at what boxing did to you."

Ali opens his eyes, raises his head. Still bent at the waist, looking deep-strong at the boy, then over at me, he motions with his left hand for me to lower my ear to his mouth. "Not the boxin'," he whispers almost intelligibly, tugging language up from the labyrinth for conceivably the very last time. "All the autograph signin'."

He points at the boy and opens his eyes wider, showing me that he wants me to tell the kid. The whites of Ali's eyes remain remarkably clear, far less yellowed than my own; his are as bright as a young child's. I tell the boy what Ali has said, recognizing that The Champ wants to make the boy (and me) feel better while having Ali-fun by plucking at the fabric of the universe, peeking underneath and giving his corner of the cosmic carpet a sweet, stiff, disrupting shake. Wiping his eyes, nose, and face on his shirt sleeve, the boy laughingly strives to dry his tears.

Yes, indeed. "There will never be another."

The Road to Mecca

Ali was actually turned down by the Army before the Army was turned down by him. He scored 78 on the IQ test, which was considered too low even for cannon

Coming hot from his Muslim conversion, this may have confirmed him in his feeling that white man's intelligence is devil's intelligence, and that there is a better

Ali inscription: "after me there will never be another"

Our Dinner with Ali

One

AS I'VE OFTEN SAID, there's little that's extraordinary about my relationship with Ali other than that it's extraordinary to me, and that I've written about him in ways no one else has. Ali has done for me more or less what he has for hundreds of thousands, if not millions, of people.

Tonight, after hanging out with Muhammad and Lonnie in their suite at the Ali Center, television and film producer Craig Mortali, newspaper and TV journalist Jon Saraceno, New York University researcher Qian Wu, and I walk to dinner at a Southern fried fish restaurant. Craig, Jon, Qian Wu, and myself: Craig calls us the "Ali Loyalists"—The Greatest of All Time has been childhood hero and adult benefactor to us all. A six-time Emmy Award winner, Craig's first major project was a sixty-minute 1994 Ali documentary; he is presently developing a documentary film for theatrical release about The Champ's legacy. Jon, who is Craig's partner on this new project, has written well and honestly about Ali more than a dozen times for various publications, particularly *USA Today*. As a professor at NYU, Qian Wu is researching and writing about Ali's influence on the almost two billion people of mainland China.

Heading up Broadway, Craig and Jon step briskly in front of Qian Wu and me. As they walk, they trade stories about their time spent with Ali, pausing to laugh at various anecdotes. I'm maybe ten years older than Jon or Craig, have a small amount of hearing loss (Kat tells me I wouldn't hear an Atlas rocket if it were launched from our backyard), and can't get close to making out every word that they're saying. By not talking, however, and by carefully listening, I manage to pull down fair-sized snatches of conversation from the chill evening air.

"So the first time I met him," Craig says, "there's a whole crew of ESPN people around. The first moment I get alone with him, I lean over and whisper in his ear, 'You've been my hero for thirty years.' Ali doesn't miss a beat. 'You're gettin' old,' he shouts where the entire room can hear it. Everybody laughs. Even though they don't know what he's talking about. Nobody'd laugh if you or I said it. He can talk about brushing your teeth and it's funny. Or about peach pie and ice cream and make it the most profound thing you'll ever hear. It doesn't matter what comes out of his mouth. If he means to be funny, it's funny; when he wants to be serious, it's serious."

After sharing nods of agreement and a laugh over Craig's story, it's Jon's turn. "'Comedy is a funny way of being serious,'" he says, quoting Ali. "'My way of joking is to tell the truth.'"

And now we're back to Craig: "So Ali opens his briefcase," Craig says, "gets out his Bible and these old beat-to-hell pieces of paper that point out discrepancies in the Bible. And he's showing them to our camera guy. And Bruce says, 'Ali, this is serious stuff. Have you ever thought about showing these to a priest?'

"'A priest?' Ali says. 'Man, I don't talk to no priest. I tell 'em to the *pope*.'"

And so, long before we reach Bob's Crab Shack on quickened legs, as if he weren't already with us, as if he hasn't been with each of us since years before we reached adolescence, Invisible Ali is walking right here among us.

As Craig opens the door and holds it for Invisible Ali and the rest of us to step through, he says, "I swear I don't think he worries like everybody else. 'It's a big world,' he says. 'The sun's always shinin' someplace.'"

✦   ✦   ✦   ✦

BOB'S CRAB SHACK. Stunningly bright overhead incandescents, ladder-backed unfinished pine chairs. The smells of fried shrimp and hush puppies, beer and sweet tea. An economy-sized extra-fat paper towel roll parked in the center of each thickly shellacked long pine table. Hooting drunks and tyrannizingly massive television screens all around us, each and every TV projecting ball games that are doing their best to compete with 1970s pop music blaring from overhead speakers. And, dominating the center of the room, a full-sized plastic replica of a red 1957 Thunderbird.

"Do people in China know Ali?" I ask Qian Wu as we're being seated.

"Everybody know Ali," he answers quickly and unhesitatingly, as if this is something he's been waiting to be asked. "Many people think he already die," he continues. And then, with a smile, "Many people think he not real, he only a legend. But everybody know Ali. Everybody."

Two

DRINKS ARE BROUGHT by our waiter, Alan. Craig asks Alan
to stay with us for a moment. Handing Alan a glass of water, Craig
raises his beer and says, "A toast."

We all lift our glasses.

"To Muhammad Ali," he says.

"May he live for ten thousand years," I offer.

We clink and drink.

Three

WE TAKE A TAXI BACK to the Galt. Qian Wu and I hop out, Craig and Jon continue to the downtown Marriott, where they're staying. Qian Wu says he has something he wants to share and asks if I'll sit with him in the lobby. As we take seats on a fat green and blue sofa, he pulls two folded pieces of paper from a trousers pocket and opens them to where I can see his triple-spaced comments. "A speech I wrote for the awards ceremony," he says and begins to read.

Mrs. Ali, Mr. Ali, distinguished guests and everyone. Good evening. I am Qian Wu from Department of Social and Cultural Analysis at New York University. It has been an honor and a pleasure to visit the Muhammad Ali Center and be here with all of you tonight.

When I first met Mrs. Ali, she asked me why as a Chinese teenager I love Mr. Ali so much. When I was in elementary school, I learned a little story about Muhammad Ali. And I was very impressed. Mr. Ali sound like a superman. And this person has influenced me from then until now. Honestly, I am not a big fan of boxing. Besides, I know boxing actually started in China one thousand years ago. However, in 1959 boxing was banned in China because people think it is dangerous. December 19, 1979, Mr. Muhammad Ali first visited China and met with Chinese chairman Deng Xiao Ping. Right after their conversation, boxing was allowed to start again in China. I don't know how Mr. Ali can do this. But he does things like this to everyone, everywhere. Mr. Ali has magic.

So, not just me, every person in China I know, they all know Ali and love him. Influenced by Ali, seven years ago I decided to study in the United States, majoring in Social and Cultural Analysis and focused on social religion. I do not love Ali as a boxer, I love Ali as a human being like everyone. This spring in India, when I visited Muhammad Ali's old friend the Dalai Lama, he told me, and I quote, "All the religions emphasize love, compassion, patience, tolerance, and forgiveness. But in today's world, the time has come to think about spirituality beyond religion altogether."

Ali is the most famous person on the planet, but I think Ali also represents the common values of human beings, something bigger than religions. I view him as a symbol beyond religion. In 1990, Muhammad Ali told his friend Davis Miller, who is also with us here tonight, "The only religion that matters is the real religion—love."

Above all of this, I just want to say thank you, Muhammad, for what you have done for the world. Thank you, Lonnie, for what you have done for Muhammad.

Sam and Isaac

One

OCTOBER 30, 2014

(the fortieth anniversary of the Foreman–Ali fight)

IN MY STUDY, FEELING THE NEED to write about Ali. Sam and I have just returned from a leaf-gathering walk. He's sitting on the floor beneath my feet, studying the largest and most obviously beautiful one: green, yellow, orange, salmon, vermilion, red, purple, and brown are each a part of this one brittle aggregate. Sam's face is lighted and radiant, round and new, uncorrupted by gravity, blond curls shimmering with morning light from a cobalt sky. How did an aged plop of protoplasm like me help create such a luminous new being?

Somehow, some way, Sam is Ali. Not figuratively. Not a reincarnation, not recycling. "There is nothing in the universe that you are not," Mawlavi Jalal al-Din wrote nearly eight hundred years ago. This ancient, formerly debatable statement, proved physically true by the all-seeing Hubble telescope in the final decade of the twentieth century, is more visibly accurate of Muhammad Ali than of anyone else I've known. In some very real sense, at least for me, Sam is a furtherance of Ali. Ali the perennially playful child, Ali the irrepressible cosmic imp. As I'm scribbling away at this idea, trying to decide if it's true, Sam is suddenly, brightly eighteen inches in front of my face, snatching my legal pad from my hands and running with it, lit up and laughing, gleefully slinging it to the floor across the far side of the room.

"It's good to have something new in your life, something that's growing," I said to new daddy Ali twenty-three and two-thirds years before. And, yes, Sam glows like Ali. Glows in a way that cannot be caught in photographs. Glows here. Glows now. Morning incandescence suffused through an opaque, sculpted, yet malleable alabaster sphere.

Two

I WALK TO THE OPEN FRONT DOOR, watch stark gold light of ozone-depleted autumn on the black-barked maple in the front yard. The dark blue color makes the sky seem further away than usual. Beside the door, the postman has left a package of bootleg Ali DVDs from a fan of my stories who lives in eastern New Jersey. I snap a disc into the player and I'm struck once again by Ali's deep and abiding innocence. Not the sham, wishful purity of purpose and action that we're so regularly imbibed with in children's movies and television, but something profound, real, troubling, and disquieting. "See my nose, look at my face," he says in a 1972 black-and-white interview for Irish television. "Most fighters have a nose like that [he squashes his with his index finger], have ears like this [pulls his away from his head and twists them to resemble cauliflower ears]. I'm pretty! And I'm the onliest fighter that can talk."

Sure, I wish that Ali would live for ten thousand years. Yet I realize that he already has: he's seen and done and been so much. "I've lived the life of one hundred men," he's told me several times, implying that there's no reason to feel bad for him. And I try my best not to.

Through Ali, the boy I once was woke from bewildering, frightening, paralyzing dreams to a world of trembling, ever-present beauty, sadness, and wonder. With Ali, the adult I've become learned about flow and mortality, time and consequence, about insanity and wisdom, about the power of play and the sapience of ridiculousness, about unbridled tenderness and stunningly finesseful violence. I can't imagine anyone whose time in the world has been more life-affirming, more life-promoting, and more excruciatingly, achingly life-revealing than that of Muhammad Ali.

Three

IN INTERVIEWS AND AMONG FRIENDS, I'm often asked what I'll remember most about Ali. Many of my memories are entirely personal and mean nothing to anyone besides me. There is one memory, though, that I believe has resonance for almost everyone.

It's 1992, and my six-year-old son, Isaac, and I are in our old Volvo, getting ready to drive back to North Carolina after a long visit with Ali at his Berrien Springs farm. It's snowing, but with little accumulation. Just enough to make the asphalt slippery. Ali has escorted us out to the car in bare shirt sleeves and slick-soled city shoes. As always, he hugs me, and this time as he does, I recognize that his touch goes through the me, past the me, to the everyone, to the everywhere.

I turn the key in the ignition. He closes our doors. There's a video camera in the backseat: I grab it and push the power button. Ali sees the camera and opens Isaac's door, snatching up my son. For a moment, as he holds Isaac for the camera, there's paramount seriousness about Ali, an intensely conscious profundity in the eyes. He wants me (and, through the electronic lens, wants each of us) to know that the care he is giving my son—and that he'll afford almost anyone's child—is of the angels. Then he blinks and, as he pulls my son higher, holding him at face level, the moment has passed.

"This is the next champion," Ali says. "This man will win the crown in 2020. Look at the face. Twenty-twenty. Just think about it: I will be the manager. I'll be ninety-three. And we will be the greatest of *that* day, the greatest of all times."

Ali places my laughing son back in his seat and points at the lens. "Watch my feet," he says in the old voice, the thick one, the one of smoke and dreams. He turns his back and takes about ten shuffling steps. There's a moment when the car engine stops, the wind doesn't move, the air is not cold.

Looking over his left shoulder, Ali raises his arms perpendicular to his sides. And although I've seen this illusion many, many times, I'm still impressed as the most famous man in the world seemingly rises from the earth once more.

Isaac held up to the camera by Ali

Lonnie

THE PHONE RINGS ONCE before she answers.

"Lonnie, hi. It's Davy. I have to tell you what my baby son just now did when he saw Muhammad."

She chuckles.

"I was reading this British newspaper article about Rasheda's sons, Biaggio and Nico, and their athletic talent. At the end of the article, there was a link to Muhammad reciting his 'I'm so fast I can run through a hurricane and not get wet' poem. My two-year-old son Sammy paid zero attention to what I was doing—until I clicked the link and Muhammad came on. The clip ran two minutes and Sammy was transfixed. When it went off, he tugged on my sleeve, saying, 'More Ali. More Ali.'

"It's his first-ever two-word sentence. The only words he says clearly are 'Mommy,' 'Daddy'—and now 'Ali.' "

She laughs big and bold. "*Soooo* cute!!! Adorable! Muhammad will be impressed. That child is extremely bright."

From Adam Until Now

Ali (*gently*): TURN YOUR CAMERA ON . . . Is it on? . . . Good . . . This is Muhammad Ali in Berrien Springs, Michigan, USA. It's the second month . . . Is that January?

Davis: February.

Ali: Today is February the eighth . . . nineteen-ninety-two. Joe Louis, Ray Robinson, they just boxers. I'm the biggest thing that ever happened in sports. I ain't boastin'; it's just the way it is. Send your astronauts up in a spaceship and have 'em write it on the moon: from Adam until now, I am the greatest in the recorded history of mankind.

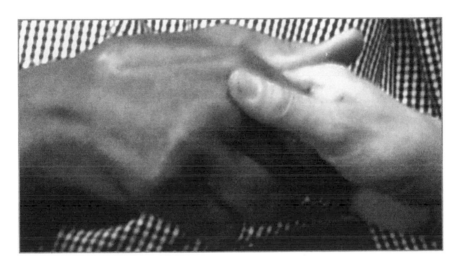

Davis's and Ali's hands, September 2014

Acknowledgments

Muhammad Ali
Yolanda Ali
Philip Marino
Bob Weil

Ike Williams
Katherine Flynn

Mike Joyce
Jamillah Ali Joyce
Gordon Marino
John Ramsey

Donald Lassere
Jeanie Kahnke
Marcel Parent
and everyone at the Muhammad Ali Center

Glenn Stout
Matthew Polly
Alex Belth

D. J. Sparr
Francesca Zambello
Michael Mael
Michael Heaston
Andrew Jorgensen
Christina Scheppelmann
Mark Campbell

Craig Mortali
Jon Saraceno
Qian Wu
Leon Gast

and especially my family:
Johanna Miller
Isaac Miller
Samuel Miller Brevard
and particularly my wife, Katherine Brevard.

And, as always, ever since 1977, Terry Davis.

Musical inspiration while I was working on this book:
Claude Debussy's *La Cathedrale Engloutie* and *Danses Sacrée et Profane*
Keith Jarrett's *La Scala, Dark Intervals, Changeless*, and *Last Solo*
Paul Simon's *Rhythm of the Saints*
Aaron Copland's *Billy the Kid* (full ballet) and "The Promise of Living" movement from the orchestral suite of *The Tender Land*

About the Author

Davis Miller is the author of the number-one international bestseller *The Tao of Muhammad Ali: A Fathers and Sons Memoir* and the number-three international bestseller *Tao of Bruce Lee: My Martial Arts Memoir*. David Halberstam and Glenn Stout judged his story "My Dinner with Ali" one of the best American sports stories of the twentieth century. Miller's fiction and nonfiction have appeared in *Esquire, Men's Journal, GQ,* and *Arena,* and in magazines published by the *Washington Post, Boston Globe, Los Angeles Times, Louisville Courier-Journal, Chicago Tribune,* (London) *Independent,* (New York) *Newsday,* and numerous other publications. His Muhammad Ali stories have been anthologized in *The Best American Sports Writing of the Century, The Best American Sports Writing 1994, The Muhammad Ali Reader,* and *The Beholder's Eye: America's Finest Personal Journalism,* among others. He is also the co-librettist of a chamber opera that is based on his transformed-by-Ali stories. He is at work on a harrowing yet comic memoir about having been recently kidnapped in China and on an obsessive modern love novel. Miller was born in Winston-Salem, North Carolina, where much of his writing takes place. He lives with his wife and son in a small wood within an hour's drive of Asheville, North Carolina.